THE
LADIES'
BOOK OF
ETIQUETTE
AND MANUAL OF
POLITENESS

T0096152

Published by Hesperus Press Limited
28 Mortimer Street, London W1W 7RD
www.hesperuspress.com

The Ladies' Book of Etiquette first published in 1860
First published by Hesperus Press Limited, 2014

Typeset and designed by Madeline Meckiffe

ISBN: 978-1-84391-542-3

THE LADIES'
BOOK OF
ETIQUETTE
AND MANUAL OF
POLITENESS

HESPERUS

CONTENTS

INTRODUCTION

I N preparing a book of etiquette for ladies, I would lay down as the first rule, 'Do unto others as you would others should do to you.' You can never be rude if you bear the rule always in mind, for what lady likes to be treated rudely? True Christian politeness will always be the result of an unselfish regard for the feelings of others, and though you may err in the ceremonious points of etiquette, you will never be impolite.

Politeness, founded upon such a rule, becomes the expression, in graceful manner, of social virtues. The spirit of politeness consists in a certain attention to forms and ceremonies, which are meant both to please others and ourselves, and to make others pleased with us; a still clearer definition may be given by saying that politeness is goodness of heart put into daily practice; there can be no *true* politeness without kindness, purity, singleness of heart, and sensibility.

Many believe that politeness is but a mask worn in the world to conceal bad passions and impulses, and to make a show of possessing virtues not really existing in the heart; thus, that politeness is merely hypocrisy and dissimulation. Do not believe this; be certain that those who profess such a doctrine are practising themselves the deceit they condemn so much. Such people scout politeness, because, to be truly a lady, one must carry the principles into every circumstance of life, into the family circle, the most intimate friendship, and never forget to extend the gentle courtesies of life to everyone. This they find too much trouble, and so deride the idea of being polite and call it deceitfulness.

True politeness is the language of a good heart, and those possessing that heart will never, under any circumstances, be rude. They may not enter a crowded saloon gracefully; they may be entirely ignorant of the *forms* of good society; they may be awkward at table, ungrammatical in speech; but they will never be heard speaking so as to wound the feelings of another; they will never be seen making others uncomfortable by seeking solely for their own *personal* convenience; they will always endeavour to set everyone around them at ease; they will be self-sacrificing, friendly, unselfish; truly in word and deed, *polite*. Give to such a woman the knowledge of the forms and customs of society, teach her how best to show the gentle courtesies of life, and you have a *lady*, created by God, only indebted for the *outward* polish to the world.

It is true that society demands this same unselfishness and courtesy, but when there is no heart in the work, the time is frittered away on the mere ceremonies, forms of etiquette, and customs of society, and this politeness seeks only its own ends; to be known as courteous, spoken of as ladylike, and not beloved as unselfish and womanly.

Etiquette exists in some form in all countries, has existed and will exist in all ages. From the rudest savage who dares not approach his ignorant, barbarous ruler without certain forms and ceremonies, to the most polished courts in Europe, or the home circles of America, etiquette reigns.

True politeness will be found, its basis in the human heart, the same in all these varied scenes and situations, but the outward forms of etiquette will vary everywhere. Even in the same scene, time will alter every form, and render the exquisite polish of last year, obsolete rudeness next year.

Politeness, being based upon real kindness of heart, cannot exist where there is selfishness or brutality to warp its growth. It is founded upon love of the neighbour, and a desire to be beloved, and to show love. Thus, where such pure, noble feelings do not exist, the mere forms of politeness become hypocrisy and deceit.

Rudeness will repel, where courtesy would attract friends.

Never by word or action notice the defects of another; be charitable, for all need charity. Remember who said, 'Let him that is without fault cast the first stone.' Remember that the laws of politeness require the consideration of the feelings of others; the endeavour to make everyone feel at ease; and frank courtesy towards all. Never meet rudeness in others with rudeness upon your own part; even the most brutal and impolite will be more shamed by being met with courtesy and kindness, than by any attempt to annoy them by insolence on your part.

Politeness forbids any display of resentment. The polished surface throws back the arrow.

Remember that a favour becomes doubly valuable if granted with courtesy, and that the pain of a refusal may be softened if the manner expresses polite regret.

Kindness, even to the most humble, will never lose anything by being offered in a gentle, courteous manner, and the most commonplace action will admit of grace and ease in its execution.

Let every action, while it is finished in strict accordance with etiquette, be, at the same time, easy, as if dictated solely by the heart.

To be truly polite, remember you must be polite at *all* times, and under *all* circumstances.

CHAPTER I

THE art of conversation consists in the exercise of two fine qualities. You must originate, and you must sympathise; you must possess at the same time the habit of communicating and of listening attentively. The union is rare but irresistible. None but an excessively ill-bred person will allow her attention to wander from the person with whom she is conversing; and especially she will never, while seeming to be entirely attentive to her companion, answer a remark or question made to another person, in another group. Unless the conversation be general among a party of friends, confine your remarks and attention entirely to the person with whom you are conversing. Steele says, 'I would establish but one great general rule in conversation, which is this – that people should not talk to please themselves, but those who hear them. This would make them consider whether what they speak be worth hearing; whether there be either wit or sense in what they are about to say; and whether it be adapted to the time when, the place where, and the person to whom, it is spoken.'

B E careful in conversation to avoid topics which may be supposed to have any direct reference to events or circumstances which may be painful for your companion to hear discussed; you may unintentionally start a subject which annoys or troubles the friend with whom you may be conversing; in that case, do not stop abruptly, when you perceive that it causes pain, and, above all, do not make the matter worse by apologising; turn to another subject as soon as possible, and pay no attention to the agitation your unfortunate remark may have excited. Many persons will, for the sake of appearing witty or smart, wound the feelings of another deeply; avoid this; it is not only ill-bred, but cruel.

R EMEMBER that having all the talk sustained by one person is not conversation; do not engross all the attention yourself, by refusing to allow another person an opportunity to speak, and also avoid the other extreme of total silence, or answering only in monosyllables.

I F your companion relates an incident or tells a story, be very careful not to interrupt her by questions, even if you do not clearly understand her; wait until she has finished her relation, and then ask any questions you may desire. There is nothing more annoying than to be so interrupted. I have heard a story told to an impertinent listener, which ran in this way:

'I saw a fearful sight –'
'When?'
'I was about to tell you; last Monday, on the train –'

'What train?'

'The train from B–. We were near the bridge –'

'What bridge?'

'I will tell you all about it, if you will only let me speak. I was coming from B–'

'Last Monday, did you say?'

and so on. The story was interrupted at every sentence, and the relator condemned as a most tedious storyteller, when, had he been permitted to go forward, he would have made the incident interesting and short.

NEVER interrupt anyone who is speaking. It is very ill-bred. If you see that a person to whom you wish to speak is being addressed by another person, never speak until she has heard and replied; until her conversation with that person is finished. No truly polite lady ever breaks in upon a conversation or interrupts another speaker.

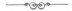

NEVER, in speaking to a married lady, enquire for her *husband*, or, if a gentleman, ask for his *wife*. The elegant way is to call the absent party by their name; ask Mr Smith how Mrs Smith is, or enquire of Mrs Jones for Mr Jones, but never for 'your husband' or 'your wife'. On the other hand, if you are married, never speak of your husband as your 'lord', 'husband', or 'good man', avoid, also, unless amongst relatives, calling him by his Christian name. If you wish others to respect him, show by speaking of him in respectful terms that you do so yourself. If either your own husband or your friend's is in the army or navy, or can claim the Dr, Prof., or any other prefix to his name, there is no impropriety in speaking of him as the colonel, doctor, or whatever his title may be.

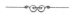

I T is a mark of ill-breeding to use French phrases or words, unless you are sure your companion is a French scholar, and, even then, it is best to avoid them. Above all, do not use any foreign word or phrase, unless you have the language perfectly at your command. I heard a lady once use a Spanish quotation; she had mastered that one sentence alone; but a Cuban gentleman, delighted to meet an American who could converse with him in his own tongue, immediately addressed her in Spanish. Embarrassed and ashamed, she was obliged to confess that her knowledge of the language was confined to one quotation.

N EVER anticipate the point or joke of any anecdote told in your presence. If *you* have heard the story before, it may be new to others, and the narrator should always be allowed to finish it in his own words. To take any sentence from the mouth of another person, before he has time to utter it, is the height of ill-breeding. Avoid it carefully.

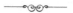

N EVER use the phrases, 'What-d-ye call it', 'Thingummy', 'What's his name', or any such substitutes for a proper name or place. If you cannot recall the names you wish to use, it is better not to tell the story or incident connected with them. No lady of high breeding will ever use these substitutes in conversation.

B E careful always to speak in a distinct, clear voice; at the same time avoid talking too loudly, there is a happy medium between mumbling and screaming. Strive to attain it.

O VERLOOK the deficiencies of others when conversing with them, as they may be the results of ignorance, and impossible to correct. Never pain another person by correcting, before others, a word or phrase mispronounced or ungrammatically constructed. If your intimacy will allow it, speak of the fault upon another occasion, kindly and privately, or let it pass. Do not be continually watching for faults, that you may display your own superior wisdom in correcting them. Let modesty and kind feeling govern your conversation, as other rules of life. If, on the other hand, your companion uses words or expressions which you cannot understand, do not affect knowledge, or be ashamed of your ignorance, but frankly ask for an explanation.

I N conversing with professional gentlemen, never question them upon matters connected with their employment. An author may communicate, voluntarily, information inter-esting to you, upon the subject of his works, but any questions from you would be extremely rude. If you meet a physician who is attending a friend, you may enquire for their progress, but do not expect him to give you a detailed account of the disease and his manner of treating it. The same rule applies to questioning lawyers about their clients, artists on their paintings, merchants or mechanics of their several branches of business. Professional or businessmen, when with ladies, generally wish for miscellaneous subjects of conversation, and, as their visits are for recreation, they will feel excessively annoyed if obliged to 'talk shop'. Still many men can converse on no other subject than their everyday employment. In this case listen politely, and show your interest. You will probably gain useful information in such conversation.

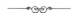

N EVER question the veracity of any statement made in general conversation. If you are certain a statement is false, and it is injurious to another person, who may be absent, you may quietly and courteously inform the speaker that he is mistaken, but if the falsehood is of no consequence, let it pass. If a statement appears monstrous, but you do not *know* that it is false, listen, but do not question its veracity. It may be true, though it strikes you as improbable.

Never attempt to disparage an absent friend. It is the height of meanness. If others admire her, and you do not, let them have their opinion in peace; you will probably fail if you try to lower her in their esteem, and gain for yourself the character of an ill-natured, envious person.

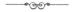

I N conversing with foreigners, if they speak slightingly of the manners of your country, do not retort rudely, or resentfully. If their views are wrong, converse upon the subject, giving them frankly your views, but never retaliate by telling them that some custom of their own country is worse. A gentleman or lady of true refinement will always give your words candid consideration, and admit that an American may possibly know the customs of her country better than they do, and if your opponent is not well bred, your rudeness will not improve his manners. Let the conversation upon national subjects be candid, and at the same time courteous, and leave him to think that the *ladies* in America are well bred, however much he may dislike some little national peculiarity.

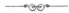

A VOID, at all times, mentioning subjects or incidents that can in any way disgust your hearers. Many persons will enter into the details of sicknesses which should be mentioned only when absolutely necessary, or describe the most revolting scenes before a room full of people, or even at table. Others speak of vermin, noxious plants, or instances of uncleanliness. All such conversation or allusion is excessively ill-bred. It is not only annoying, but absolutely sickening to some, and a truly ladylike person will avoid all such topics.

I CANNOT too severely censure the habit of using sentences which admit of a double meaning. It is not only ill-bred, but indelicate, and no person of true refinement will ever do it. If you are so unfortunate as to converse with one who uses such phrases, never by word, look, or sign show that you under-stand any meaning beyond the plain, outspoken language.

A VOID always any discussion upon religious topics, unless you are perfectly certain that your remarks cannot annoy or pain anyone present. If you are tête-à-tête with a friend, and such a discussion arise, enquire your companion's church and mention your own, that you may yourself avoid unpleasant remarks, and caution him.

———◦✐◦———

N EVER, when advancing an opinion, assert positively that a thing '*is so*', but give your opinion *as* an opinion. Say, 'I think this is so,' or 'these are *my* views,' but remember that your companion may be better informed upon the subject under discussion, or, where it is a mere matter of taste or feeling, do not expect that all the world will feel exactly as you do.

———◦✐◦———

N EVER repeat to a person with whom you converse, any unpleasant speech you may have heard concerning her. If you can give her pleasure by the repetition of a delicate compliment, or token of approval shown by a mutual friend, tell her the pleasant speech or incident, but do not hurt her feelings, or involve her in a quarrel by the repetition of ill-natured remarks.

———◦✐◦———

A MONGST well-bred persons, every conversation is considered in a measure confidential. A lady or gentleman tacitly confides in you when he (or she) tells you an incident which may cause trouble if repeated, and you violate a confidence as much in such a repetition, as if you were bound over to secrecy. Remember this.

NEVER criticise a companion's dress, or indeed make any remark whatever upon it. If a near friend, you may, if sincere, admire any article, but with a mere acquaintance let it pass unnoticed. If, however, any accident has happened to the dress, of which she is ignorant, tell her of it, and assist her in repairing the mischief.

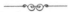

To be able to converse really well, you must read much, treasure in your memory the pearls of what you read; you must have a quick comprehension, observe passing events, and listen attentively whenever there is any opportunity of acquiring knowledge. A quick tact is necessary, too, in conversation. To converse with an entirely uneducated person upon literature, interlarding your remarks with quotations, is ill-bred. It places them in an awkward situation, and does not add to your popularity. In conversing with persons of refinement and intelligence, do not endeavour to attract their admiration by pouring forth every item of your own information upon the subject under consideration, but listen as well as talk, and modestly follow their lead. I do not mean, to assent to any opinion they may advance, if you really differ in your own tastes, but do not be *too* ready to show your superior judgement or information. Avoid argument; it is not conversation, and frequently leads to ill feeling. If you are unfortunately drawn into an argument, keep your temper under perfect control, and if you find your adversary is getting too warm, endeavour to introduce some other topic.

———⚬◉⚬———

A VOID carefully any allusion to the age or personal defects of your companion, or anyone who may be in the room, and be very careful in your language when speaking of a stranger to another person. I have heard a lady enquire of a gentleman, 'who that frightful girl in blue could be', and receive the information that the lady in question was the gentleman's own sister.

———⚬◉⚬———

B E careful, when travelling, not to wound the feelings of your friends in another country or city, by underrating their native place, or attempting to prove the superiority of your own home over theirs.

———⚬◉⚬———

V ERY young girls are apt to suppose, from what they observe in older ones, that there is some particular manner to be put on, in talking to gentlemen, and, not knowing exactly what it is, they are embarrassed and reserved; others observe certain airs and looks, used by their elders in this intercourse, and try to imitate them, as a necessary part of company behaviours, and, so become affected, and lose that first of charms, simplicity, natural grace. To such, let me say, your companions are in error; it requires no peculiar manner, nothing to be put on, in order to converse with gentlemen, any more than with ladies; and the more

pure and elevated your sentiments are, and the better cultivated your intellect is, the easier will you find it to converse
pleasantly with all. One good rule can be always followed by
young ladies; to converse with a lady friend as if there were
gentlemen present, and to converse with a gentleman as if in
the room with other ladies.

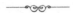

AVOID affectation; it is the sure test of a deceitful, vulgar
mind. The best cure is to try to have those virtues which
you would affect, and then they will appear naturally.

CHAPTER II

Dress

'A LADY is never so well dressed as when you cannot remember what she wears.'

No truer remark than the above was ever made. Such an effect can only be produced where every part of the dress harmonises entirely with the other parts, where each colour or shade suits the wearer's style completely, and where there is perfect neatness in each detail. One glaring colour, or conspicuous article, would entirely mar the beauty of such a dress. It is, unfortunately, too much the custom in America to wear any article, or shape in make, that is fashionable, without any regard to the style of the person purchasing goods. If it is the fashion it must be worn, though it may greatly exaggerate a slight personal defect, or conceal or mar what would otherwise be a beauty. It requires the exercise of some judgement to decide how far an individual may follow the dictates of fashion, in order to avoid the appearance of eccentricity, and yet wear what is peculiarly becoming to her own face or figure. Another fault of our fair countrywomen is their extravagance in dress. No better advice can be given to a young person than to dress always according to her circumstances. She will be more respected with a simple wardrobe, if it is known either that she is dependent upon her own exertions for support, or is saving a husband or father from unnecessary outlay, than if she wore the most costly fabrics, and by so doing incurred debt or burdened her relatives with heavy, unwarrantable expense. If neatness, consistency, and good taste, preside over the wardrobe of a lady, expensive fabrics will not be needed; for with the simplest materials, harmony of colour, accurate fitting to the figure, and perfect neatness, she will always appear well dressed.

GENERAL RULES
Neatness

This is the first of all rules to be observed with regard to dress. Perfect cleanliness and careful adjustment of each article in the dress are indispensable in a finished toilet. Let the hair be always smooth and becomingly arranged, each article exquisitely clean, neat collar and sleeves, and tidy shoes and stockings, and the simplest dress will appear well, while a torn or soiled collar, rough hair, or untidy feet will entirely ruin the effect of the most costly and elaborate dress. The many articles required in a lady's wardrobe make a neat arrangement of her drawers and closets necessary, and also require care in selecting and keeping goods in proper order. A fine collar or lace, if tumbled or soiled, will lose its beauty when contrasted with the same article in the coarsest material perfectly pure and smooth. Each article of dress, when taken off, should be placed carefully and smoothly in its proper place.

Adaptiveness

Let each dress worn by a lady be suitable to the occasion upon which she wears it. A toilet may be as offensive to good taste and propriety by being too elaborate, as by being slovenly. Never wear a dress which is out of place or out of season under the impression that 'it will do for once', or 'nobody will notice it'. It is in as bad taste to receive your morning calls in an elaborate evening dress, as it would be to attend a ball in your morning wrapper.

Harmony

To appear well dressed without harmony, both in colour and materials, is impossible. When arranging any dress, whether for home, street, or evening, be careful that each colour harmonises well with the rest, and let no one article, by its glaring costliness, make all the rest appear mean. A costly lace worn over a thin, flimsy silk, will only make the dress appear poorer, not, as some suppose, hide its defects. A rich trimming looks as badly upon a cheap dress, as a mean one does upon an expensive fabric. Observe this rule always in purchasing goods. One costly article will entirely ruin the harmony in a dress, which, without it, though plain and inexpensive, would be becoming and beautiful. Do not save on the dress or cloak to buy a more elaborate bonnet, but let the cost be well equalised and the effect will be good. A plain merino or dark silk, with a cloth cloak, will look much better than the most expensive velvet cloak over a cheap delaine dress.

Fashion

Do not be too submissive to the dictates of fashion; at the same time avoid oddity or eccentricity in your dress. There are some persons who will follow, in defiance of taste and judgement, the fashion to its most extreme point; this is a sure mark of vulgarity. Every new style of dress will admit of adaptation to individual cases, thus producing a pleasing, as well as fashionable effect. Not only good taste, but health is often sacrificed to the silly error of dressing in the extreme of fashion. Be careful to have your dress comfortable and becoming, and let the prevailing mode come into secondary consideration; avoiding, always, the other extreme of oddity or eccentricity in costume.

Style and Form of Dress

Be always careful when making up the various parts of your wardrobe, that each article fits you accurately. Not in the outside garments alone must this rule be followed, an ill-fitting pair of corsets, or wrinkles in any other article of the underclothes, will make a dress set badly, even if it has been itself fitted with the utmost accuracy. A stocking which is too large, will make the boot uncomfortably tight, and too small will compress the foot, making the shoe loose and untidy. In a dress, no outlay upon the material will compensate for a badly fitting garment. A cheap calico made to fit the form accurately and easily, will give the wearer a more ladylike air than the richest silk which either wrinkles or is too tightly strained over the figure. Collars or sleeves, pinned over or tightly strained to meet, will entirely mar the effect of the prettiest dress.

Economy

And by economy I do not mean mere cheapness. To buy a poor, flimsy fabric merely because the price is low, is extravagance, not economy; still worse if you buy articles because they are offered cheap, when you have no use for them. In purchasing goods for the wardrobe, let each material be the best of its kind.

The same amount of sewing that is put into a good material, must be put into a poor one, and, as the latter will very soon wash or wear out, there must be another one to supply its place, purchased and made up, when, by buying a good article at first, this time and labour might have been saved. A good, strong material will be found cheapest in the end, though the actual expenditure of money may be larger at first.

Comfort

Many ladies have to trace months of severe suffering to an improper disregard of comfort, in preparing their wardrobe, or in exposure after they are dressed. The most exquisite ball costume will never compensate for the injury done by tight lacing, the prettiest foot is dearly paid for by the pain a tight boot entails, and the most graceful effects will not prevent suffering from exposure to cold. A light ball dress and exquisite arrangement of the hair, too often make the wearer dare the inclemency of the coldest night, by wearing a light shawl or hood, to prevent crushing delicate lace or flowers. Make it a fixed rule to have the head, feet, and chest well protected when going to a party, even at the risk of a crushed flower or a stray curl. Many a fair head has been laid in a coffin, a victim to consumption, from rashly venturing out of a heated ballroom, flushed and excited, with only a light protection against keen night air. The excitement of the occasion may prevent immediate discomfort in such cases, but it adds to the subsequent danger.

Details

Be careful always that the details of your dress are perfectly finished in every point. The small articles of a wardrobe require constant care to keep in perfect order, yet they will woefully revenge themselves if neglected. Let the collar, hand-kerchief, boots, gloves, and belts be always whole, neat, and adapted to the dress. A lace collar will look as badly over a chintz dress, as a linen one would with velvet, though each may be perfect of its kind. Attention to these minor points are sure tests of taste in a lady's dress. A shabby or ill-fitting boot or glove will ruin the most elaborate walking dress, while one of much plainer make and coarser fabric will be becoming and ladylike, if all the details are accurately fitted, clean, and well put on. In arranging a dress for every occasion, be careful that there is no missing string, hook, or button, that the folds hang well, and that every part is even and properly adjusted.

HOME DRESSES
Morning Dress

The most suitable dress for breakfast is a wrapper made to fit the figure loosely, and the material, excepting when the winter weather requires woollen goods, should be of chintz, gingham, brilliante, or muslin. A lady who has children, or one accustomed to perform for herself light household duties, will soon find the advantage of wearing materials that will wash. A large apron of domestic gingham, which can be taken off, if the wearer is called to see unexpected visitors, will protect the front of the dress, and save washing the wrapper too frequently. If a lady's domestic duties require her attention for several hours in the morning, whilst her list of acquaintances is large, and she has frequent morning calls, it is best to dress for callers before breakfast, and wear over this dress a loose sack and skirt of domestic gingham. This, while protecting the dress perfectly, can be taken off at a moment's notice if callers are announced. Married ladies often wear a cap in the morning, and lately, young girls have adopted the fashion. It is much better to let the hair be perfectly smooth, requiring no cap, which is often worn to conceal the lazy, slovenly arrangement of the hair. A few moments given to making the hair smooth and presentable without any covering, will not be wasted. Slippers of embroidered cloth are prettiest with a wrapper, and in summer black morocco is the most suitable for the house in the morning.

Dress for Morning Visits

A lady should never receive her morning callers in a wrapper, unless they call at an unusually early hour, or some unexpected demand upon her time makes it impossible to change her dress after breakfast. On the other hand, an elaborate costume before dinner is in excessively bad taste. The dress should be made to fit the figure neatly, finished at the throat and wrists by an embroidered collar and cuffs, and, unless there is a necessity for it, in loss of the hair or age, there should be no cap or headdress worn. A wrapper made with handsome trimming, open over a pretty white skirt, may be worn with propriety; but the simple dress worn for breakfast, or in the exercise of domestic duties, is not suitable for the parlour when receiving visits of ceremony in the morning.

Evening Dress

The home evening dress should be varied according to circumstances. If no visitor is expected, the dress worn in the morning is suitable for the evening; but to receive visitors, it should be of lighter material, and a light headdress may be worn. For young ladies, at home, ribbon or velvet are the most suitable materials for a headdress. Flowers, unless they be natural ones in summer, are in very bad taste, excepting in cases where a party of invited guests are expected. Dark silk in winter, and thin material in summer, make the most suitable dresses for evening, and the reception of the chance-guests ladies in society may usually expect.

Walking Dresses

Walking dresses, to be in good taste, should be of quiet colours, and never conspicuous. Browns, modes, and neutral tints, with black and white, make the prettiest dresses for the street. Above all, avoid wearing several bright colours. One may be worn with perfect propriety to take off the sombre effect of a dress of brown or black, but do not let it be too glaring, and wear but little of it. Let the boots be sufficiently strong and thick to protect the feet from damp or dust, and wear always neat, clean, nicely fitting gloves. The entire effect of the most tasteful costume will be ruined if attention is not paid to the details of dress. A soiled bonnet cap, untidy strings, or torn gloves and collar will utterly spoil the prettiest costume. There is no surer mark of vulgarity than over dressing or gay dressing in the street. Let the materials be of the costliest kind, if you will, but do not either wear the exaggerations of the fashion, or conspicuous colours. Let good taste dictate the limits where fashion may rule, and let the colours harmonise well, and be of such tints as will not attract attention.

Shopping Dresses

Should be of such material as will bear the crush of a crowded store without injury, and neither lace or delicate fabrics should ever be worn. A dress of merino in winter, with a cloth cloak and plain velvet or silk bonnet is the most suitable. In summer, a dress and cloak of plain mode-coloured Lavella cloth, or any other cool but strong fabric, with a simply trimmed straw bonnet, is the best dress for a shopping excursion.

Storm Dresses

A lady who is obliged to go out frequently in bad weather, will find it both a convenience and economy to have a storm dress. Both dress and cloak should be made of a woollen material (varying of course with the season) which will shed water. White skirts are entirely out of place, as, if the dress is held up, they will be in a few moments disgracefully dirty. A woollen skirt, made quite short, to clear the muddy streets, is the proper thing. Stout, thick-soled boots, and gloves of either silk, beaver-cloth, or lisle thread, are the most suitable. The bonnet should be either of straw or felt, simply trimmed; and, above all, carry a *large* umbrella. The little light umbrellas are very pretty, no doubt, but to be of any real protection in a storm, the umbrella should be large enough to protect the whole dress.

Marketing

Here a dress of the most inexpensive kind is the best. There is no surer mark of vulgarity, than a costly dress in the market. A chintz is the best skirt to wear, and in winter a dark chintz skirt put on over a delaine dress, will protect it from baskets, and the unavoidable soils contracted in a market, while it looks perfectly well, and can be washed if required.

Travelling

Travelling dresses should be made always of some quiet colour, perfectly plain, with a deep mantle or cloak of the same material. When travelling with a young babe, a dress of material that will wash is the best, but it should be dark and plain. A conspicuous travelling dress is in very bad taste, and jewellery or ornaments of any kind are entirely out of place. Let the dress be made of dark, plain material, with a simple straw or felt bonnet, trimmed with the same colour as the dress, and a thick barège veil. An elastic string run through a tuck made in the middle of the veil, will allow one half to fall over the face, while the other half falls back, covering the bonnet, and protecting it from dust. If white collars and sleeves are worn, they should be of linen, perfectly plain. Strong boots and thick gloves are indispensable in travelling, and a heavy shawl should be carried, to meet any sudden change in the weather. Corsets and petticoats of dark linen are more suitable than white ones, as there is so much unavoidable dust and mud constantly meeting a traveller.

Evening Dresses

Must be governed by the number of guests you may expect to meet, and the character of the entertainment to which you are invited. For small social companies, a dark silk in winter, and a pretty lawn, barège, or white muslin in summer, are the most appropriate. A light headdress of ribbon or velvet, or a plain cap, are the most suitable with this dress. For a larger party, low-necked, short-sleeved silk, light coloured, or any of the thin goods made expressly for evening wear, with kid gloves, either of a colour to match the dress or of white; black lace mittens are admissible, and flowers in the hair. A ball dress should be made of either very dressy silk, or light, thin material made over silk. It should be trimmed with lace, flowers, or ribbon, and made dressy. The *coiffure* should be elaborate, and match the dress, being either of ribbon, feather, or flowers. White kid gloves, trimmed to match the dress, and white or black satin slippers, with silk stockings, must be worn.

Mourning

There is such a variety of opinion upon the subject of mourning, that it is extremely difficult to lay down any general rules upon the subject. Some wear very close black for a long period, for a distant relative; whilst others will wear dressy mourning for a short time in a case of death in the immediate family. There is no rule either for the depth of mourning, or the time when it may be laid aside, and I must confine my remarks to the different degrees of mourning.

For deep mourning, the dress should be of bombazine, Parramatta cloth, delaine, barège, or merino, made up over black lining. The only appropriate trimming is a deep fold, either of the same material or of crape. The shawl or cloak must be of plain black, without border or trimming, unless a fold of crape be put on the cloak; the bonnet should be of crape, made perfectly plain, with crape facings, unless the widow's cap be worn, and a deep crape veil should be thrown over both face and bonnet. Black crape collar and sleeves, and black boots and gloves.

CHAPTER III

Travelling

THERE is no situation in which a lady is more exposed than when she travels, and there is no position where a dignified, ladylike deportment is more indispensable and more certain to command respect. If you travel under the escort of a gentleman, give him as little trouble as possible; at the same time, do not interfere with the arrangements he may make for your comfort. It is best, when starting upon your journey, to hand your escort a sufficient sum of money to cover all your expenses, retaining your pocket book in case you should wish to use it. Have a strong pocket made in your upper petticoat, and in that carry your money, only reserving in your dress pocket a small sum for incidental expenses. In your travelling satchel carry an oilskin bag, containing your sponge, tooth and nail brushes, and some soap; have also a calico bag, with hairbrush and comb, some pins, hairpins, a small mirror, and some towels. In this satchel carry also some crackers, or sandwiches, if you will be long enough upon the road to need a luncheon.

IN your carpet bag, carry a large shawl, and if you will travel by night, or stop where it will be inconvenient to open your trunks, carry your night clothes, and what clean linen you may require, in the carpet bag. It is best to have your name and address engraved upon the plate of your carpet bag, and to sew a white card, with your name and the address to which you are travelling, in clear, plain letters upon it. If you carry a novel or any other reading, it is best to carry the book in your satchel, and not open the carpet bag until you are ready for the night. If you are to pass the night in the cars, carry a warm woollen or silk hood, that you may take off your bonnet at night. No one can sleep comfortably in a bonnet. Carry also, in this case, a large shawl to wrap round your feet.

O NE rule to be always observed in travelling is punctuality. Rise early enough to have ample time for arranging everything needful for the day's journey. If you sleep upon the boat, or at a hotel, always give directions to the servant to waken you at an hour sufficiently early to allow ample time for preparation. It is better to be all ready twenty minutes too soon, than five minutes late, or even late enough to be annoyed and heated by hurrying at the last moment.

A LADY will always dress plainly when travelling. A gay dress, or finery of any sort, when in a boat, stage, or car, lays a woman open to the most severe misconstruction. Wear always neutral tints, and have the material made up plainly and substantially, but avoid carefully any article of dress that is glaring or conspicuous. Above all, never wear jewellery (unless it be your watch) or flowers; they are both in excessively bad taste. A quiet, unpretending dress, and dignified demeanour, will ensure for a lady respect, though she travel alone from Maine to Florida.

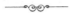

IF you are obliged to pass the night upon a steamboat secure, if possible, a stateroom. You will find the luxury of being alone, able to retire and rise without witnesses, fully compensates for the extra charge. Before you retire, find out the position and number of the stateroom occupied by your escort, in case you wish to find him during the night. In times of terror, from accident or danger, such care will be found invaluable.

WHEN in the car if you find the exertion of talking painful, say so frankly; your escort cannot be offended. Do not continually pester either your companion or the conductor with questions, such as 'Where are we now?' 'When shall we arrive?' If you are wearied, this impatience will only make the journey still more tedious. Try to occupy yourself with looking at the country through which you are passing, or with a book.

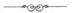

IF you are travelling without any escort, speak to the conductor before you start, requesting him to attend to you whilst in the car or boat under his control. Sit quietly in the cars when they reach the depot until the first bustle is over, and then engage a porter to procure for you a hack, and get your baggage. If upon a boat, let one of the servants perform this office, being careful to fee him for it. Make an engagement with the hackman, to take you only in his hack, and enquire his charge before starting. In this way you avoid unpleasant company during your drive, and overcharge at the end of it.

I F you expect a friend to meet you at the end of your journey, sit near the door of the steamboat saloon, or in the ladies' room at the car depot, that he may find you easily.

I N travelling alone, choose, if possible, a seat next to another lady, or near an elderly gentleman. If your neighbour seems disposed to shorten the time by conversing, do not be too hasty in checking him. Such acquaintances end with the journey, and a lady can always so deport herself that she may beguile the time pleasantly, without, in the least, compromising her dignity.

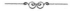

A N Y slight attention, or an apology made for crushing or incommoding you, is best acknowledged by a courteous bow, in silence.

CHAPTER IV

How to Behave at a Hotel

IN America, where the mania for travelling extends through all classes, from the highest to the lowest, a few hints upon deportment at a hotel will not be amiss, and these hints are especially addressed to ladies travelling alone.

WHEN you arrive at the hotel, enquire at once for the proprietor. Tell him your name and address, and ask him to conduct you to a good room, naming the length of time you purpose occupying it. You may also request him to wait upon you to the table, and allot you a seat. As the hours for meals, at a large hotel, are very numerous, it is best to mention the time when you wish to breakfast, dine, or sup. If you stay more than one day at the hotel, do not tax the proprietor with the duty of escorting you to the table more than once.

REQUEST one of the waiters always to meet you as you enter, and wait upon you to your seat. This saves the embarrassment of crossing the room entirely unattended, while it shows others that you are a resident at the house. The waiter will then take your order for the dishes you wish. Give this order in a low tone, and do not harass the man by contradicting yourself several times; decide what you want before you ask for it, and then give your order quietly but distinctly. Use, always, the butter-knife, salt-spoon, and sugar-tongs, though you may be entirely alone in the use of them. The attention to the small details of table etiquette is one of the surest marks of good breeding. If any trifling civility is offered by the gentleman beside you, or opposite to you, thank him civilly, if you either accept or decline it. Thank the waiter for any extra attention he may offer.

R EMEMBER that a ladylike deportment is always modest and quiet. If you meet a friend at table, and converse, let it be in a tone of voice sufficiently loud for him to hear, but not loud enough to reach ears for which the remarks are not intended. A boisterous, loud voice, loud laughter, and bold deportment, at a hotel, are sure signs of vulgar breeding.

W HEN you have finished your meal, cross the room quietly; if you go into the parlour, do not attract attention by a hasty entrance, or forward manner, but take the seat you may select, quietly.

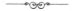

T HE acquaintances made in a hotel may be dropped afterwards, if desirable, without rudeness, and a pleasant greeting to other ladies whom you may recognise from meeting them in the entries or at table, is courteous and well bred; be careful, however, not to force attentions where you see they are not agreeably received.

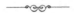

AFTER breakfast, pass an hour or two in the parlour, unless you are going out, whilst the chambermaid puts your room in order. You should, before leaving the room, lock your trunk, and be careful not to leave money or trinkets lying about. When you go out, lock your door, and give the key to the servant to hand to the clerk of the office, who will give it to you when you return. You may do this, even if you leave the room in disorder, as the chambermaids all carry duplicate keys, and can easily enter your room in your absence to arrange it. The door should not be left open, as dishonest persons, passing along the entry, could enter without fear of being questioned.

IF you see that another lady, though she may be an entire stranger, is losing her collar, or needs attention called to any disorder in her dress, speak to her in a low tone, and offer to assist her in remedying the difficulty.

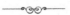

NEVER sit down to the piano uninvited, unless you are alone in the parlour. Do not take any book you may find in the room away from it.

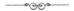

I N a strange city it is best to provide yourself with a small map and guide book, that you may be able to find your way from the hotel to any given point, without troubling anyone for directions.

I F you wish for a carriage, ring, and let the waiter order one for you.

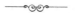

W HEN leaving a hotel, if you have been there for several days, give the waiter at table, and the chambermaid, a fee, as your unprotected situation will probably call for many services out of their regular routine of duties.

O N leaving, ring, order your bill, pay it, state the time at which you wish to leave, and the train you will take to leave the city. Request a man to be sent, to carry your baggage to the hack; and if you require your next meal at an unusual hour, to be ready for your journey, order it then.

CHAPTER V

Evening Parties

ETIQUETTE FOR THE HOSTESS

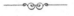

T HE most fashionable as well as pleasant way in the present day, to entertain guests, is to invite them to evening parties, which vary in size from the 'company', 'sociable', 'soirée', to the party, *par excellence*, which is but one step from the ball.

T HE entertainment upon such occasions may vary with the taste of the hostess, or the caprice of her guests. Some prefer dancing, some music, some conversation. Small parties called together for dramatic or poetical readings, are now fashionable, and very delightful.

I N writing an invitation for a small party, it is kind, as well as polite, to specify the number of guests invited, that your friends may dress to suit the occasion. To be either too much, or too little dressed at such times is embarrassing.

For large parties, the usual formula is:

> *Miss S-- 's compliments to Miss G--,*
> *and requests the pleasure of her company for*
> *Wednesday, March 8th, at 8 o 'clock.*

Such an invitation, addressed either to an intimate friend or mere acquaintance, will signify full dress.

———

If your party is a musical soirée, or your friends meet for reading or conversation alone, say so in your invitation, as –

> *Miss S-- requests the pleasure of Miss G-- 's*
> *company, on Thursday evening next, at 8 o 'clock,*
> *to meet the members of the musical club, to which*
> *Miss S-- belongs;*

or,

> *Miss S-- expects a few friends, on Monday*
> *evening next, at 8 o 'clock, to take part in some*
> *dramatic readings, and would be happy to have*
> *Miss G-- join the party.*

Always date your note of invitation, and put your address in one corner.

———

Having dispatched these notes, the next step is to prepare to receive your guests. If the number invited is large, and you hire waiters, give them notice several days beforehand, and engage them to come in the morning. Give them full directions for the supper, appoint one to open the door, another to show the guests to the dressing rooms, and a third to wait in the gentlemen's dressing room, to attend to them, if their services are required.

If you use your own plate, glass, and china, show the waiters where to find them, as well as the tablecloths, napkins, and other things they may require. If you hire the service from the confectioner's or restaurateur's where you order your supper, you have only to show your waiters where to spread supper, and tell them the hour.

You will have to place at least four rooms at the disposal of your guests – the supper room, and two dressing rooms, beside the drawing room.

In the morning, see that the fires in your rooms are in good order; and in the drawing room, it is best to have it so arranged that the heat can be lessened towards evening, as the crowd, and dancing, will make it excessively uncomfortable if the rooms are too warm. See that the lights are in good order, and if you propose to have music instead of dancing, or to use your piano for dancing music, have it put in good tune in the morning. If you intend to dance, and do not wish to take up the carpets, you will find it economical, as well as much pleasanter, to cover them with coarse white muslin or linen; be sure it is fastened down smoothly, firmly, and drawn tightly over the carpets.

Do not remove all the chairs from the parlour; or, if this is necessary, leave some in the hall, for those who wish to rest after dancing.

In the dining room, unless it will accommodate all your guests at once, have a silk cord so fastened that, when the room is full, it can be drawn across the doorway; those following the guests already in the room, will then return to the parlour, and wait their turn. A still better way, is to set the supper table twice, inviting the married and elderly people to go into the first table, and then, after it is ready for the second time, let the young folks go up.

Two dressing rooms must be ready; one for the ladies, and the other for the gentlemen. Have both these rooms comfortably heated, and well lighted. Nothing can be more disagreeable than cold, ill-lighted rooms to dress in, particularly if your guests come in half-frozen by the cold of a winter's night, or still worse, damp from a stormy one.

B E sure that there is plenty of water, soap and towels on the washstand, two or three brushes and combs on the bureau, two mirrors, one large and one small, and a pin cushion, well filled with large and small pins.

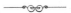

I N the ladies' room, have one, or if your party is large, two women to wait upon your guests; to remove their cloaks, overshoes, and hoods, and assist them in smoothing their dresses or hair. After each guest removes her shawl and hood, let one of the maids roll all the things she lays aside into a bundle, and put it where she can easily find it. It is an admirable plan, and prevents much confusion, to pin to each bundle, a card, or strip of paper (previously prepared) with the name of the person to whom it belongs written clearly and distinctly upon it.

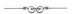

U PON the bureau in the ladies' room, have a supply of hairpins, and a workbox furnished with everything requisite to repair any accident that may happen to the dress of a guest. It is well, also, to have Eau de Cologne, hartshorn, and salts, in case of sudden faintness.

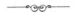

I N the gentlemen's room, place a clothes brush and boot-jack.

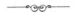

I T is best to send out your invitations by your own servant, or one hired for that purpose especially. It is ill-bred to send invitations either by the dispatch, or through the post office; and besides being discourteous, you risk offending your friends, as these modes of delivery are proverbially uncertain.

———◦◦◦———

B E dressed and ready to receive your guests in good season, as some, in their desire to be punctual, may come before the time appointed. It is better to be ready too soon, than too late, as your guests will feel painfully embarrassed if you are not ready to receive them.

———◦◦◦———

F OR the early part of the evening, take a position in your parlour, near or opposite to the door, that each guest may find you easily. It is not necessary to remain all the evening nailed to this one spot, but stay near it until your guests have all or nearly all assembled. Latecomers will of course expect to find you entertaining your guests.

———◦◦◦———

A S each guest or party enter the room, advance a few steps to meet them, speaking first to the lady, or if there are several ladies, to the eldest, then to the younger ones, and finally to the gentlemen. If the newcomers are acquainted with those already in the room, they will leave you, after a few words of greeting, to join their friends; but if they are strangers to the city, or making their first visit to your house, introduce them to a friend who is well acquainted in your circle, who will entertain them till you can again join them and introduce them to others.

DO not leave the room during the evening. To see a hostess fidgeting, constantly going in and out, argues ill for her tact in arranging the house for company. With well-trained waiters, you need give yourself no uneasiness about the arrangements outside of the parlours.

THE perfection of good breeding in a hostess, is perfect ease of manner; for the time she should appear to have no thought or care beyond the pleasure of her guests.

HAVE a waiter in the hall to open the front door, and another at the head of the first flight of stairs, to point out to the ladies and gentlemen their respective dressing rooms.

NEVER try to outshine your guests in dress. It is vulgar in the extreme. A hostess should be dressed as simply as is consistent with the occasion, wearing, if she will, the richest fabrics, exquisitely made, but avoiding any display of jewels or gay colours, such as will be, probably, more conspicuous than those worn by her guests.

R EMEMBER, from the moment your first guest enters the parlour, you must forget yourself entirely to make the evening pleasant for others. Your duties will call you from one group to another, and require constant watchfulness that no one guest is slighted. Be careful that none of the company are left to mope alone from being unacquainted with other guests. Introduce gentlemen to ladies, and gentlemen to gentlemen, ladies to ladies.

I T requires much skill and tact to make a party for conversation only, go off pleasantly. You must invite only such guests as will mutually please, and you must be careful about introductions. If you have a literary lion upon your list, it is well to invite other lions to meet him or her, that the attention may not be constantly concentrated upon one person. Where you see a couple conversing slowly and wearily, stir them up with a few sprightly words, and introduce a new person, either to make a trio, or, as a substitute in the duet, carrying off the other one of the couple to find a more congenial companion elsewhere. Never interrupt an earnest or apparently interesting conversation. Neither party will thank you, even if you propose the most delightful substitute.

I F your party meet for reading, have a table with the books in the centre of the apartment, that will divide the room, those reading being on one side, the listeners on the other. Be careful here not to endeavour to shine above your guests, leaving to them the most prominent places, and taking, cheerfully, a subordinate place. On the other hand, if you are urged to display any talent you may possess in this way, remember your only desire is to please your guests, and if they are really desirous to listen to you, comply, gracefully and promptly, with their wishes.

I F you have dancing, and have not engaged a band, it is best to hire a pianist for the evening to play dancing music. You will find it exceedingly wearisome to play yourself all the evening, and it is ill-bred to ask any guest to play for others to dance. This victimising of some obliging guest is only too common, but no true lady will ever be guilty of such rudeness. If there are several members of the family able and willing to play, let them divide this duty amongst them, or, if you wish to play yourself, do so. If any guest, in this case, offers to relieve you, accept their kindness for *one* dance only. Young people, who enjoy dancing, but who also play well, will often stay on the piano stool all the evening, because their own good nature will not allow them to complain, and their hostess wilfully, or through negligence, permits the tax.

S EE that your guests are well provided with partners, introducing every gentleman and lady who dances, to one who will dance well with them. Be careful that none sit still through your negligence in providing partners.

D O not dance yourself, when, by so doing, you are preventing a guest from enjoying that pleasure. If a lady is wanted to make up a set, then dance, or if, late in the evening, you have but few lady dancers left, but do not interfere with the pleasure in others. If invited, say that you do not wish to take the place of a guest upon the floor, and introduce the gentleman who invites you to some lady friend who dances.

I T is very pleasant in a dancing party to have ices *alone*, handed round at about ten o'clock, having supper set two or three hours later. They are very refreshing, when it would be too early to have the more substantial supper announced.

I T is very customary now, even in large parties, to have no refreshments but ice cream, lemonade, and cake, or, in summer, fruit, cake, and ices. It is less troublesome, as well as less expensive, than a hot supper, and the custom will be a good one to adopt permanently.

O NE word of warning to all hostesses. You can never know, when you place wine or brandy before your guests, whom you may be tempting to utter ruin. Better, far better, to have a reputation as strict, or mean, than by your example, or the temptation you offer, to have the sin upon your soul of having put poison before those who partook of your hospitality. It is not necessary; hospitality and generosity do not require it, and you will have the approval of all who truly love you for your good qualities, if you resolutely refuse to have either wine or any other intoxicating liquor upon your supper-table.

I F the evening of your party is stormy, let a waiter stand in the vestibule with a *large* umbrella, to meet the ladies at the carriage door, and protect them whilst crossing the pavement and steps.

W HEN your guests take leave of you, it will be in the drawing room, and let that farewell be final. Do not accompany them to the dressing room, and never stop them in the hall for a last word. Many ladies do not like to display their 'sortie du soirée' before a crowded room, and you will be keeping their escort waiting. Say farewell in the parlour, and do not repeat it.

I F your party is mixed, that is, conversation, dancing, and music are all mingled, remember it is your place to invite a guest to sing or play, and be careful not to offend any amateur performers by forgetting to invite them to favour the company. If they decline, never urge the matter. If the refusal proceeds from unwillingness or inability on that occasion, it is rude to insist; and if they refuse for the sake of being urged, they will be justly punished by a disappointment. If you have guests who, performing badly, will expect an invitation to play, sacrifice their desire to the good of the others, pass them by. It is torture to listen to bad music.

D o not ask a guest to sing or play more than once. This is her fair share, and you have no right to tax her too severely to entertain your other guests. If, however, the performance is so pleasing that others ask for a repetition, then you too may request it, thanking the performer for the pleasure given.

CHAPTER VI

---❦---

Evening Parties

ETIQUETTE FOR THE GUEST

U PON receiving an invitation for an evening party, answer it immediately, that your hostess may know for how many guests she must provide. If, after accepting an invitation, any unforeseen event prevents your keeping the engagement, write a second note, containing your regrets. The usual form is –

Miss G-- accepts with pleasure Miss S-- 's polite invitation for Monday next

or,

Miss G-- regrets that a prior engagement will prevent her accepting Miss S-- 's kind invitation for Monday evening

---❦---

P UNCTUALITY is a mark of politeness, if your invitation states the hour at which your hostess will be ready to welcome you. Do not be more than half an hour later than the time named, but if unavoidably detained, make no apology when you meet your hostess; it will be in bad taste to speak of your want of punctuality.

WHEN you arrive at your friend's house, do not stop to speak to anyone in the hall, or upon the stairs, but go immediately to the dressing room. The gentleman who accompanies you will go to the door of the ladies' room, leave you, to remove his own hat and overcoat, and then return to the door to wait for you.

IN the dressing room, do not push forward to the mirror if you see that others are before you there. Wait for your turn, then perform the needful arrangements of your toilette quickly, and rejoin your escort as soon as possible. If you meet friends in the ladies' room, do not stop there to chat; you keep your escort waiting, and your friends will join you in the parlour a few moments later.

AVOID all confidential communications or private remarks in the dressing room. You may be overheard, and give pain or cause annoyance by your untimely conversation.

WHEN you enter the parlour, go immediately to your hostess, and speak to her; if the gentleman attending you is a stranger to the lady of the house, introduce him, and then join the other guests, as by delaying, to converse too long with your hostess, you may prevent her speaking to others who have arrived later than yourself.

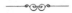

IF you have no escort, you may with perfect propriety send for the master of the house, to wait upon you from the dressing room to the parlour, and as soon as you have spoken to the hostess, thank your host and release him, as the same attention may be required by others. Again, when alone, if you meet a friend in the dressing room, you may ask the privilege of entering the parlour with her and her escort; or, if she also is alone, there is no impropriety in *two* ladies going into the room unattended by a gentleman.

WHILE you maintain a cheerful deportment, avoid loud talking and laughing, and still more carefully avoid any action or gesture that may attract attention and make you conspicuous.

WHEN dressing for a party, while you show that you honour the occasion by a tasteful dress, avoid glaring colours, or any conspicuous ornament or style of costume.

AVOID long tête-à-tête conversations; they are in bad taste, and to hold confidential communication, especially with gentlemen, is still worse.

DO not make any display of affection for even your dearest friend; kissing in public, or embracing, are in bad taste. Walking with arms encircling waists, or such demonstrative tokens of love, are marks of low breeding.

AVOID crossing the room alone, and never run, even if you feel embarrassed, and wish to cross quickly.

IF you are a musician, and certain that you will confer pleasure by a display of your talents, do not make a show of reluctance when invited to play or sing. Comply gracefully, and after one piece, leave the instrument. Be careful to avoid the appearance of wishing to be invited, and, above all, never hint that this would be agreeable. If your hostess has requested you to bring your notes, and you are dependent upon them, bring them, and quietly place them on the music stand, or, still better, send them in the afternoon. It is a better plan, if you are called upon frequently to contribute in this way to the evening's amusement, to learn a few pieces so as to play them perfectly well without notes.

NEVER attempt any piece before company, unless you are certain that you can play it without mistake or hesitation. When you have finished your song or piece, rise instantly from the piano stool, as your hostess may wish to invite another guest to take the place. If you have a reason for declining to play, do so decidedly when first invited, and do not change your decision.

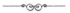

IF your hostess or any of the family play for the guests to dance, it is both polite and kind to offer to relieve them; and if truly polite themselves, they will not take advantage of the offer, to *over*tax your good nature.

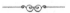

WHEN others are playing or singing, listen quietly and attentively; to laugh or talk loudly when there is music in the room, is rude, both toward the performer and your hostess. If you are conversing at the time the music begins, and you find that your companion is not disposed to listen to the performer at the harp or piano, converse in a low tone, and take a position at some distance from the instrument.

IF the rooms are not large enough for all the guests to dance at one time, do not dance every set, even if invited. It is ill-bred and selfish.

WHEN you go up to supper, do not accept anything from any gentleman but the one who has escorted you from the parlour. If others offer you, as they probably will, any refreshment, say that Mr — (naming your escort) has gone to get you what you desire. He has a right to be offended, if, after telling him what you wish for, he returns to find you already supplied. It is quite as rude to offer what he brings to another lady. Her escort is probably on the same errand from which yours has just returned.

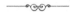

IT may seem trivial and childish to warn a lady against putting cakes or bonbons in her pocket at supper, yet it is often done by those who would deeply resent the accusation of rudeness or meanness. It is not only ill-bred, but it gives rise, if seen, to suspicions that you are so little accustomed to society, or so starved at home, that you are ignorant of the forms of etiquette, or are forced to the theft by positive hunger.

IF you are obliged to leave the company at an earlier hour than the other guests, say so to your hostess in a low tone, when you have an opportunity, and then stay a short time in the room, and slip out unperceived. By a formal leave-taking, you may lead others to suppose the hour later than it is in reality, and thus deprive your hostess of other guests, who, but for your example, would have remained longer. French leave is preferable to a formal leave-taking upon such occasions.

I F you remain until the usual hour for breaking up, go to your hostess before you leave the room, express the pleasure you have enjoyed, and bid her farewell.

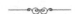

W ITHIN the next week, you should call upon your hostess, if it is the first party you have attended at her house. If she is an intimate friend, the call should be made within a fortnight.

CHAPTER VII

Visiting

ETIQUETTE FOR THE HOSTESS

WHEN you write to invite a friend to visit you, name a time when it will be convenient and agreeable for you to receive her, and if she accepts your invitation, so arrange your duties and engagements that they will not interfere with your devoting the principal part of your time to the entertainment of your guest. If you have certain duties which must be performed daily, say so frankly when she first arrives, and see that during the time you are so occupied she has work, reading, music, or some other employment, to pass the time away pleasantly.

HAVE a room prepared especially for her use, and let her occupy it alone. Many persons have a dislike to anyone sleeping with them, and will be kept awake by a companion in the room or bed. Above all, do not put a child to sleep in the chamber with your guest.

THE day before your friend arrives, have her room swept, dusted, and aired; put clean, fresh linen upon the bed, see that the curtains are in good order, the locks in perfect repair, and the closet or wardrobe and bureau empty for her clothes. Have upon the bureau a pin cushion well filled, hairpins, brush and comb, and two mirrors, one large, and one small for the hand, as she may wish to smooth her hair, without unpacking her own toilet articles. Upon the wash-stand, have two pitchers full of water, a cup, tumbler, soap-dish and soap, basin, brush-dish, and a sponge, wash rag, and plenty of clean towels.

HAVE both a feather bed and a mattress upon the bedstead, that she may place whichever she prefers uppermost. Two sheets, a blanket, quilt, and counterpane, should be on the bed, and there should be two extra blankets in the room, should she require more covering in the night.

ON the mantelpiece, place a few books that she may read, if she wishes, before sleeping. Have upon the mantel-piece a box of matches, and if the room is not lighted by gas, have also a supply of candles in a box, and a candlestick.

IF the room is not heated by a furnace, be careful that the fire is made every morning before she rises, and keep a good supply of fuel in the room. Besides the larger chairs, have a low one, to use while changing the shoes or washing the feet.

U PON the table, place a full supply of writing materials, as your guest may wish to send word of her safe arrival before unpacking her own writing-desk. Put two or three postage stamps upon this table.

B E sure that bells, locks, hinges, and windows, are all in perfect order.

B EFORE your guest arrives, go to her room. If it is in winter, have a good fire, hot water on the washstand, and see that the windows are tightly closed, and the room cheerful with sunshine, or plenty of candle or gas light. If in summer, draw the curtains, bow the shutters, open the windows, and have a fan upon the table. It is well to have a bath ready, should your guest desire that refreshment after the dust and heat of travelling.

W HEN the time arrives at which you may expect your guest, send a carriage to the station to meet her, and, if possible, go yourself, or send some member of the family to welcome her there. After her baggage is on the carriage, drive immediately to the house, and be certain all is ready there for her comfort.

As soon as she is at your house, have her trunks carried immediately to her own room, and lead her there yourself. Then, after warmly assuring her how welcome she is, leave her alone to change her dress, bathe, or lie down if she wishes. If her journey has been a long one, and it is not the usual hour for your next meal, have a substantial repast ready for her about half an hour after her arrival, with tea or coffee.

If she arrives late at night, after she has removed her bonnet and bathed her face, invite her to partake of a substantial supper, and then pity her weariness and lead the way to her room. She may politely assert that she can still sit up and talk, but be careful you do not keep her up too long; and do not waken her in the morning. After the first day, she will, of course, desire to breakfast at your usual hour, but if she has had a long, fatiguing journey, she will be glad to sleep late the first day. Be careful that she has a hot breakfast ready when she does rise, and take a seat at the table to wait upon her.

After the chambermaid has arranged the guest-chamber in the morning, go in yourself and see that all is in order, and comfortable, and that there is plenty of fresh water and towels, the bed properly made, and the room dusted. Then do not go in again through the day, unless invited. If you are constantly running in, to put a chair back, open or shut the windows, or arrange the furniture, you will entirely destroy the pleasantest part of your guest's visit, by reminding her that she is not at home, and must not take liberties, even in her own room. It looks, too, as if you were afraid to trust her, and thought she would injure the furniture.

I F you have children, forbid them to enter the room your friend occupies, unless she invites them to do so, or they are sent there with a message.

I F your household duties will occupy your time for some hours in the morning, introduce your guest to the piano, bookcase, or picture-folio, and place all at her service. When your duties are finished, either join her in her own room, or invite her to sit with you, and work, chatting, meanwhile, together. If you keep your own carriage, place it at her disposal as soon as she arrives.

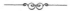

I F she is a stranger in the city, accompany her to the points of interest she may wish to visit, and also offer to show her where to find the best goods, should she wish to do any shopping.

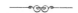

E NQUIRE of your visitor if there is any particular habit she may wish to indulge in, such as rising late, retiring early, lying down in the daytime, or any other habit that your family do not usually follow. If there is, arrange it so that she may enjoy her peculiarity in comfort. If there is any dish which is distasteful to her, avoid placing it upon the table during her visit, and if she mentions, in conversation, any favourite dish, have it frequently placed before her.

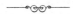

I F she is accustomed to eat just before retiring, and your family do not take supper, see that something is sent to her room every night.

I F your friend has intimate friends in the same city, beside yourself, it is an act of kindly courtesy to invite them to dinner, tea, or to pass a day, and when calls are made, and you see that it would be pleasant, invite the caller to remain to dinner or tea.

N EVER accept any invitation, either to a party, ball, or public entertainment, that does not include your guest. In answering the invitation give that as your reason for declining, when another note will be sent enclosing an invitation for her. If the invitation is from an intimate friend, say, in answering it, that your guest is with you, and that she will accompany you.

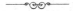

I T is a mistaken idea to suppose that hospitality and courtesy require *constant* attention to a guest. There are times when she may prefer to be alone, either to write letters, to read, or practise. Some ladies follow a guest from one room to another, never leaving them alone for a single instant, when they would enjoy an hour or two in the library or at the piano, but do not like to say so.

THE best rule is to make your guest feel that she is heartily welcome, and perfectly at home.

WHEN she is ready to leave you, see that her trunks are strapped in time by the servants, have a carriage ready to take her to the station, have the breakfast or dinner at an hour that will suit her, prepare a luncheon for her to carry, and let some gentleman in the family escort her to the wharf, check her trunks, and procure her tickets.

CHAPTER VIII

Visiting

ETIQUETTE FOR THE GUEST

As a first rule with regard to paying a visit, the best one is, never to accept a *general* invitation. Instances are very common where women (I cannot say *ladies*) have, upon a slight acquaintance, and a 'When you are in C— I should be very happy to have you visit me,' actually gone to C— from their own home, and, with bag and baggage, quartered themselves upon the hospitality of their newly made friend, for weeks at a time.

Even where there is a long-standing friendship it is not well to visit uninvited. It is impossible for you, in another city, to know exactly when it will be convenient for your friend to have you visit her, unless she tells you, and that will, of course, be a special invitation.

If your friends are really desirous to have you pay them a visit, they will name a time when it will be convenient and agreeable to have you come, and you may accept the invitation with the certainty that you will not incommode them.

SELF-PROPOSED visits are still worse. You, in a manner, force an invitation from your friend when you tell her that you can come at a certain time, unless you have previously arranged to let her know when you can be her guest. In that case, your own time is understood to be the most agreeable for her.

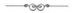

IF, whilst travelling, you pass through a town where you have friends whom you wish to visit, and who would be hurt if you omitted to do so, go first to a hotel, and either call or send word that you are there. Then, it is optional with them to extend their hospitality or not. Do not be offended if it is not done. The love for you may be undiminished, and the desire to entertain you very great, yet family reasons may render such an invitation as you expect, impossible. Your friend may have engagements or duties at the time, that would prevent her making the visit pleasant for you, and wish to postpone the invitation until she can entertain you as she wishes.

TO drive, trunks and all, in such a case, to your friend's house, without a word of warning, is unkind, as well as ill-bred. You force her to invite you to stay, when it may be inconvenient, and, even if she is really glad to see you, and wishes you to make a prolonged visit, you may feel certain she would have preferred to know you were coming. If she really loves you, her natural desire would be to have everything ready to give you a comfortable reception, and not have to leave you, perhaps with your travelling costume on, for an hour or two, while she prepares a room for you. It is not enough to say, at such a time, 'Don't mind me', or, 'Treat me as one of the family'. However much her politeness or love may conceal annoyance, be sure, in her secret heart she *does* mind you, and remember you are *not* one of her private family.

T o take the liberty of going to the house of a mere acquaintance, for a night or two, while travelling, without invitation, is making a convenience of them, and wears the appearance of wishing to save the customary hotel bill, so, while it is extremely ill-bred and impertinent, it is also excessively mean.

I n case of relationship, or long intimate friendship, an unexpected visit may be pardoned and give pleasure, but it is better to avoid it, as the pleasure will surely be increased if your relative or friend has time to prepare for your reception as her love will prompt, and arrange her duties and engagements to really enjoy your company.

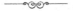

W hen you receive an invitation by letter to visit a friend, answer it immediately, thanking her for her proffered hospitality, and say decidedly then whether you can accept or decline.

I F you accept the invitation, state in your letter by what train, and at what hour you will arrive, that she may meet you, and let nothing but positive necessity keep you from being punctually at the time and place appointed. To linger by the way, for mere pleasure, and make her come several times to meet you, is unkind, as well as ill-bred. If you are unavoidably detained, write to her, state the reason that will prevent your keeping the appointment, and name another time when you can come.

I T is well in answering a letter of invitation, to state the limits of your visit, and then to keep them. If she is unwilling to let you go, and you are tempted to stay, that very fact promises well for the pleasure of a second visit. It is better to leave while all will regret you, than to linger on until you have worn out your welcome.

E NQUIRE, as soon as possible after your arrival, what are the regular habits of the family; the hours for rising, for meals, and for retiring, and then be punctual in your attendance. Many ladies are very ceremonious about waiting for a guest, and by delay in your room, or inattention to the time, when you are out, you will keep the whole family waiting.

I F you do not wake early enough for the usual breakfast hour, request the chambermaid to knock at your door in time for you to be ready to go down with the family. Before you leave your room in the morning, take the clothes off your bed, throw the upper bed over the foot-board, and then open all the windows (unless it storms), that room and bed may be thoroughly aired before you sit there again.

A FTER breakfast, ask your hostess if you can be of any assistance to her in the household duties. If she declines your services, do not follow her from room to room whilst she is thus engaged, but take your work, books, or music to the sitting room or parlour, until your own room is ready for you. By thus proving that you can occupy yourself pleasantly, while she is away, you make it less annoying to her to feel the obligation to leave you.

A s soon as you see that she is ready to sew and chat, leave your book, or, if in your own room, come to the sitting room, where she is, and work with her. It is polite and kind, if you see that she has a large supply of family sewing, to offer to assist her, but if she positively declines your aid, then have some work of your own on hand, that you may sew with her. Many pleasant mornings may be spent while visiting, by one lady reading aloud whilst the other sews, alternating the work.

I T is a pretty compliment to repay the hospitality of your hostess, by working whilst with her upon some piece of fancy work, a chair cover, sofa cushion, or pair of ottomans, presenting them to her when finished, as a keepsake. They will be duly appreciated, and remind her constantly of the pleasures of your visit.

I F you pass the morning out of the house, remember your time is hers, and have no engagement to interfere with the plans she has laid for entertaining you. Observe this rule during your whole visit, and do not act independent of her plans. By constantly forming engagements without her knowledge, going out without her, or staying in when she has made some excursion or party for your pleasure, you insult her, by intimating that her house is no more to you than a hotel, to sleep and eat in, while your pleasures lie elsewhere.

A FTER dinner, retire for an hour to your own room, that your hostess may lie down if she is accustomed to do so. If the hours kept are later than you have been accustomed to, or if the gaiety of the family keeps you out at party or opera, it is best to sleep after dinner, even if you do not always do it. To give signs of weariness in the evening will be excessively rude, implying want of enjoyment, and making your hostess feel hurt and annoyed.

I F you have shopping to do, find out where the best stores are, and then go to them alone, unless your hostess will accompany you upon similar business of her own. Do not tax her good nature to go, merely for the sake of aiding you as guide. If one of the children in the family is familiar with the stores and streets, ask her to accompany you, and be careful to acknowledge the kindness by buying something especially for the child whilst she is out with you, if it is only some cakes or bonbons. Choose an hour when you are certain your hostess has made no other engagement for you, or while she is busy in her domestic duties, for these shopping excursions. Offer, when you are going, to attend to any shopping she may want, and ask if there is any commission you can execute for her while you are out.

W HILE on a visit to one friend, do not accept too many invitations from others, and avoid spending too much time in paying calls where your hostess is not acquainted. You owe the greater portion of your time and society to the lady whose hospitality you are accepting, and it is best to decline invitations from other houses, unless they enclose one for your hostess also.

A VOID paying any visits in a family not upon good terms with your hostess. If such a family are very dear friends of your own, or you can claim an acquaintance, pleasant upon both sides, with them, write, and state candidly the reason why you cannot visit them, and they will appreciate your delicacy.

I F, while on a visit to one friend, you receive an invitation to spend some time with another friend in the same place, accept it for the period which you have named as the termination of your first visit. You insult your hostess by shortening your visit to her to accept another invitation, and quite as much of an insult is it, to take the time from the first visit to go to pay another, and then return to your first hostess, unless such an arrangement has been made immediately upon your arrival.

N EVER invite any friend who may call upon you to stay to dinner or tea; you will be taking a most unwarrantable liberty in so doing. This is the right of your hostess, and if, by her silence, she tacitly declines extending this courtesy, you will be guilty of impertinence in usurping her privilege.

N EVER take anyone who calls upon you into any room but the parlour, unless invited to do so by your hostess. You have, of course, the *entrée* of other rooms, but you have no right to extend this privilege to others.

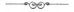

I F you have many gentlemen visitors, check too frequent calls, and make no appointments with them. If they show you any such attention as to offer to drive you to places of interest, or visit with you picture galleries or public places, always consult your hostess before accepting such civilities, and decline them if she has made other engagements for you. If you receive an invitation to visit any place of public amusement, decline it, unless one of the family with whom you are staying is also invited. In that case you may accept. If the gentleman who invites you is a stranger to the family, introduce him to your hostess, or mention her name in conversation. He will then, if he really desires you to accept his proffered attention, include her in the invitation.

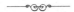

WHEN visiting in a family where the members are in mourning, decline all invitations to parties or places of public amusement. It is an insult to them to leave them to join in pleasure from which their recent affliction excludes them. Your visit at such a time will be prompted by sympathy in their trouble, and for the time it is thoughtful and delicate to make their sorrows yours.

IF sudden sickness or family trouble come to your friend whilst you are with her, *unless you can really be useful*, shorten your visit. In time of trouble families generally like to be alone, all in all to each other; and a visitor is felt a constant restraint.

IF death comes while you are with your friend, endeavour to take from her as much of the care as you can, a really sympathising friend is an inexpressible comfort at such a time, as the trying details which must be taken in charge by someone, will be less trying to her than to a member of the family. Do the necessary shopping for your friend, and relieve her of as much family care as you can. Let her feel that you are really glad that you are near her in her affliction, and repay the hospitality she offered in her season of joy by showing her that her sorrow makes her still more dear, and that, while you can enjoy the gaiety of her house, you will not flee from its mourning. When your presence can be of no further service, then leave her.

PUT out your washing and ironing when on a visit. It is annoying and ill-bred to throw your soiled clothes into the family wash.

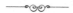

TAKE with you, from home, all the writing and sewing materials you may require while paying your visit. It is annoying to be constantly requested by a visitor to lend her scissors, pins, needles, or paper; no lady should be without her own portfolio and work-box.

BE very careful not to injure any article of furniture in your sleeping apartment, and if, unfortunately, anything suffers from your carelessness, have the accident repaired, or the article replaced, at your own expense.

WHEN your visit is over, give a present to each of the servants, varying its value, according to the length of your visit or the services you may have required. You will add to the pleasure by presenting such gifts yourself, with a few pleasant words.

NEVER compare the house you may be visiting with your own, or any other you may visit. Avoid also speaking of any house where you may have been a guest in terms of over-praise, giving glowing pictures of its splendour. Your hostess may imagine you are drawing comparisons unfavourable to your present residence. Also avoid speaking unfavourably of any former visit, as your hostess will naturally conclude that her turn for censure will come as soon as your visit is over.

IF any family secret comes to your knowledge while you are on a visit in that family, remember the hospitality extended to you binds you to the most inviolable secrecy. It is mean, contemptible, rude, and ill-bred to make your enter-tainers regret their hospitality by betraying any such confidence; for it is as sacred a confidence as if you were bound over to silence in the most solemn manner.

AFTER paying a visit, you should write to your hostess as soon as you reach home again; thank her in this letter for her hospitality, speak warmly of the enjoyment you have had in your recent visit, and mention by name every member of the family, desiring to be remembered to all.

CHAPTER IX

Morning Receptions or Calls
ETIQUETTE FOR THE HOSTESS

I F your circle of visiting acquaintance is very large, while at the same time your time is fully occupied, or your home duties make it inconvenient to dress every morning to receive visitors, it is a good plan to set aside one morning in the week for a reception day.

U PON your own visiting cards, below the name, put the day when it will be proper to return the visit, thus:

> Mrs JAMES HUNTER.
> *at home*
> WEDNESDAYS.
> No. 1718 C— St.

Y OUR friends will, unless there is some especial reason for a call in the interval, pay their visit upon the day named.

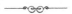

L ET nothing, but the most imperative duty, call you out upon your reception day. Your callers are, in a measure, invited guests, and it will be an insulting mark of rudeness to be out when they call. Neither can you be excused, except in case of sickness.

H AVING appointed the day when you will be at home to see your friends, you must, for that day, prepare to give your time wholly to them. The usual hours for morning receptions are from twelve to three, and you should be dressed, and ready for callers, at least half an hour before that time.

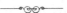

T O come in, flushed from a hurried toilette, to meet your first callers, is unbecoming as well as rude.

Y OUR dress should be handsome, but not showy. A silk or cashmere wrapper, richly trimmed, over an embroidered skirt, with a pretty cap, or the hair neatly arranged without headdress, is a becoming and appropriate dress. Still better is a rich but plain silk, made high in the neck, with long sleeves. Wear a handsomely embroidered, or lace collar, and sleeves, and a rather dressy cap, or, still better, the hair alone, prettily arranged.

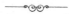

As each visitor arrives, rise, and advance part of the way to meet her. If gentlemen, rise, but do not advance.

It is not customary now to introduce callers at these morning receptions, though you can do so with perfect propriety where you know such an introduction will be agreeable to both parties.

In introducing a gentleman to a lady, address her first, as –

'Miss Jones, permit me to introduce Mr Lee;'

and, when introducing a young lady to a matron, you introduce the younger one to the elder, as –

'Mrs Green, allow me to introduce to you my friend, Miss Brown.'

In introducing strangers in the city it is well to name the place of their residence, as – Mr James of Germany, or, Mr Brown of New York, or, if they have recently returned from abroad, it is well to say so, as, Mr Lee, lately from India; this is useful in starting conversation.

B E careful, when introducing your friends, to pronounce the name of each one clearly and distinctly, that there may be no mistake or necessity for repetition.

I T is a good plan, if your receptions are usually largely attended, to have books and pictures on the centre table, and scattered about your parlours. You must, of course, converse with each caller, but many will remain in the room for a long time, and these trifles are excellent pastime, and serve as subjects for conversation.

I T requires much tact to know when to introduce friends, when to take refuge under the shield fashion offers, and not make them acquainted with each other. It is a positive cruelty to force a talented, witty person, to converse with one who is ignorant and dull, as they will, of course, be obliged to do, if introduced.

A WELL-BRED lady, who is receiving several visitors at a time, pays equal attention to all, and attempts, as much as possible, to generalise the conversation, turning to all in succession. The last arrival, however, receives a little more attention at first, than the others.

I F it is not agreeable to you to set aside a day for the especial reception of callers, and you have a large circle of acquaintances, be ready to receive them each day that you are at home.

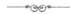

I F you are engaged, let the servant say so when she opens the door, and do not send down that message after your friend has been admitted. If she is told when she arrives that you are engaged, she will understand that you are denied to *all* callers, but if that message comes after she has sent up her card, she may draw the inference that you will not see *her*, though you may see other friends.

N EVER keep a caller waiting whilst you make an elaborate toilette. If you are not ready for visitors, it is best to enter the parlour in your wrapper, apologising for it, than to keep your friend waiting whilst you change your dress.

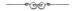

I F a stranger calls, bringing a letter of introduction, and sends the letter, you may read it before going downstairs, but if they wait till you are in the parlour before presenting the letter, merely glance at the signature and at the name of your caller; do not read the letter through, unless it is very short, or you are requested by the bearer to do so.

I F you have a friend staying with you, invite her to join you in the parlour when you have callers, and introduce her to your friends.

I F you wish to invite a caller to stay to luncheon or dinner, give the invitation as soon as you have exchanged greetings, not after she has been seated for some time. In the latter case it appears like an afterthought, not, as in the former, as if from a real desire to have the pleasure of her company.

I F you have but one caller at a time, rise when she does, and accompany her to the vestibule; but, if there are several in the room, rise when each one does, but only accompany them to the parlour door; there take leave of them, and return to those who still remain seated.

I F, after affliction, your friends call before you are able to see them, do not fear to give offence by declining to receive them. They will respect your sorrow, and the call is made more to show their sympathy than from a desire to converse with you.

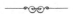

V ISITS of condolence, paid between the death of one of your family and the day of the funeral, you may always excuse yourself from, with perfect propriety. They are made in kindness, and show interest, but if you decline seeing such callers, there is no offence given.

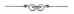

I N parting from a gentleman caller, rise when he does, and remain standing until he leaves the room, but do not go towards the door.

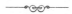

W HEN a gentleman calls in the morning he will not remove his outside coat, and will hold his hat in his hand. Never offer to take the latter, and do not invite him to remove his coat. Take no notice of either one or the other.

I F strangers in the city call upon you, enquire at what hotel they are staying, and how long they will be there, that you may return their call before they leave town.

CHAPTER X

Morning Receptions or Calls

ETIQUETTE FOR THE CALLER

T HE usual hours for paying morning calls are between eleven and two, or twelve and three, and all calls of ceremony should be made between these hours.

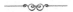

N EVER, in paying a ceremonious call, stay more than twenty minutes, or less than ten. If your hostess has several other visitors at the same time that you are in her parlour, make your visit short, that she may have more attention to bestow upon others.

A FTER you have received an invitation to a party, call within a week or fortnight after the evening, whether you have accepted or declined the invitation. If you have declined on account of mourning, the excuse extends also to the call.

W HEN the servant answers your ring, hand in your card.
If your friend is out or engaged, leave the card, and if
she is in, send it up. Never call without cards. You may offend
your friend, as she may never hear of your call, if she is out
at the time, and you trust to the memory of the servant.

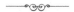

I F your friend is at home, after sending your card up to
her by the servant, go into the parlour to wait for her.
Sit down quietly, and do not leave your seat until you rise
to meet her as she enters the room. To walk about the
parlour, examining the ornaments and pictures, is ill-bred.
It is still more unladylike to sit down and turn over to read
the cards in her card basket. If she keeps you waiting for a
long time, you may take a book from the centre-table to pass
away the interval.

N EVER, while waiting in a friend's parlour, go to the
piano and play till she comes. This is a breach of good-
breeding often committed, and nothing can be more ill-bred.
You may be disturbing an invalid unawares, or you may
prevent your friend, if she has children, from coming downstairs at all, by waking the baby.

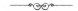

I F you are a stranger in the city, and bring a letter of introduction to your hostess, send this letter upstairs with your
card, that she may read it, and know how to welcome you
when she comes downstairs. In this case, write upon the card

the name of the hotel at which you are staying, and mention
in the course of conversation, how long you will be in the city.

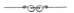

I F you have a visitor, and desire to introduce her to your
friends, you may invite her to accompany you when
paying calls.

I N making a call for condolence, it is sufficient to leave a
card with your enquiries for the health of your friend, and
offers of service. The same if calling upon invalids, if they
are too ill to see you.

I N visits of congratulation, go in, and be hearty in your
expressions of interest and sympathy. Pay visits, both of
condolence and congratulation, within a week after the event
which calls for them occurs.

I N paying your visits of condolence, show, by your own
quiet gravity, that you sympathise in the recent affliction
of your friend. Though you may endeavour to comfort and
cheer her, you must avoid a gay or careless air, as it will be
an insult at such a time. Avoid any allusion to the past that
may be trying for her to hear or answer, yet do not ignore
the subject entirely, as that appears like a want of interest
in it. Though you may feel happy, avoid parading your own

joyousness at such a time; whatever your own feeling may be, respect the sorrow of another.

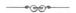

NEVER sit gazing curiously around the room when paying a call, as if taking a mental inventory of the furniture. It is excessively rude. It is still worse to appear to notice any disorder or irregularity that may occur.

IF, while paying a call, you perceive that any unforeseen matter in the family, calls for the attention of the lady of the house, leave instantly, no matter how short your call has been. Your friend may not appear to notice the screams of a child, a noise in the kitchen, or the cry from the nursery that the fire board has caught fire, but you may be sure she does hear it, and though too well bred to speak of it, will heartily rejoice to say goodbye.

DO not take a child with you to pay calls, until it is old enough to behave quietly and with propriety. To have a troublesome child constantly touching the parlour ornaments, balancing itself on the back of a chair, leaning from a window, or performing any of the thousand tricks in which children excel, is an annoyance, both to yourself and your hostess.

MAKE no remark upon the temperature of the room, or its arrangement, when you enter it. Never open or shut a window or door without asking permission, and unless really suffering from excessive heat or cold, refrain from asking leave to take this liberty.

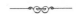

I F you are invited to go upstairs to your friend's private apartment, you will, of course, accept the invitation, but never go upstairs uninvited. When you reach her door, if the servant has not preceded and announced you, knock, and await her invitation to enter. Then, once in, take no notice of the room, but go instantly to your friend. If she is sewing, do not speak of the nature of her work, but request her to continue, as if you were not present.

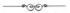

I N cases of long standing friendship, you will not, of course, stand upon the ceremony of waiting for each and every one of your calls to be returned before paying another, but be careful that you are not too lavish of your visits. The most cordial welcome may be worn threadbare, if it is called into use *too* often.

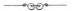

I F you are visiting an invalid, or one confined by physical infirmity to one apartment, while you are cheerful and ready to impart all the news that will interest them, do not, by too glowing descriptions of outdoor pleasures, make them feel more keenly their own deprivations. It is well, when making such calls, to converse upon literature, or such general subjects as will not remind them of their misfortune.

I N cases where, from long illness or other infirmity, a gentleman friend is confined entirely to his room, you may, with perfect propriety, call upon him. It is both polite and kind to do so, as otherwise he would be deprived entirely of the society of his lady friends. Many thus unfortunately situated, from study and reading while so shut out from the world, become the most delightful companions.

I F, when you make a call, you unfortunately intrude upon an early dinner hour, do not go in, but leave your card, and say that you will call again.

I F you call upon two ladies who are boarding at the same house, do not send up your card to both at the same time. If one is out, send a card to her room, and then send up for the other. If the first one is in, wait till she comes down, and then chat as long as a call usually lasts. When you rise as if to take leave, accompany your friend to the parlour door, then tell her that you are going to send up for your other friend. She will bid you good morning, and go to her own room; ring the bell after she leaves you, and send your card by the waiter to your other friend.

CHAPTER XI

———◦◦◦———

Dinner Company

ETIQUETTE FOR THE HOSTESS

IN issuing invitations for a large dinner party, the usual form is –

Mr and Mrs G—
request the favour of
Mr and Mrs L—'s
company to dinner,
on Wednesday, March 8th,
at– o'clock.

———◦◦◦———

IF your husband is giving a party to gentlemen only, he will have a card printed or written for the occasion, but your duties as hostess, if he wishes you to preside, will still be as arduous as if your own friends were included in the invitation.

———◦◦◦———

THE directions given in the chapter on 'Evening Parties' for the arrangement of the parlour and the dressing rooms, will apply here equally well, but the dining room (in this case the centre of attraction) requires still more careful attention. Any fault here will mar your own comfort and the pleasure of your guests, and must be carefully avoided.

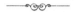

SEND out your invitations by a servant, or man hired for the purpose; do not trust them to despatch or penny post.

BE careful in selecting the guests for a dinner party. Remember that conversation will be the sole entertainment for several hours, and if your guests are not well chosen, your dinner, no matter how perfect or costly the viands, will prove a failure. The most agreeable dinners are those whose numbers will allow all the guests to join in a common conversation, and where the host has spirit and intelligence to take the lead, and start a new subject when the interest in the old one begins to flag. Dinners where the guests depend entirely upon the person next them for conversation, are apt to be stupid, as it requires marvellous tact to pair off all the couples, so that everyone will be entertaining in tête-à-tête conversation.

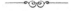

TO give a good dinner, your means, room, and establishment must all be taken into consideration when you are preparing for a dinner company. If you invite a large number, you must increase your establishment for the occasion, as to sit down to a dinner badly served, with a scarcity of waiters, is tiresome, and shows little tact or grace on the part of the hostess.

ONE cook cannot prepare dinner properly for more than ten persons, and three waiters will find ample employment in waiting upon the same number. More than this number will require a table too large for general, easy conversation, and throw your company into couples or trios, for entertainment.

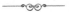

HAVE your table spread in a room that will accom-modate all the guests comfortably, at the same time avoid putting a small social party in a large room, where they will appear lost in the space around them. Let the room be comfortably warmed, and if your dinner is late, have the apartments well lighted. If you sit down by daylight, but will remain in the room until after dark, have the shutters closed and the lights lit, before the dinner is announced, as nothing can be more awkward than to do this in the middle of the meal.

THE shape of a table is a point of more importance than some people think. If you wish your dinner to be social – not a mere collection of tête-à-têtes – the table should be of a shape which will make it easy for each guest to address anyone at the table. The long parallelogram, with the host at one end and the hostess at the other, is stiff, too broad, too long, and isolates the givers of the feast from the guests.

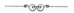

THE round table, if large enough to accommodate many guests, has too large a diameter each way for easy conversation. The best table is the oval, and the host and hostess should sit in the middle of each side, facing each other.

THE dining room, even in the heat of summer, should be carpeted, to deaden the noise of the servants' feet. The chairs should be easy, without arms, and with tall, slanting backs. It adds much to the comfort, if each person is provided with a footstool.

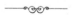

YOU must have, besides the waiters, one servant to carve, and he must be an adept. No dish should be carved upon the table, and that no guest shall wait too long for his meat, you must engage a rapid and dexterous carver.

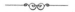

FOR a party of ten, two waiters, and the carver, are amply sufficient. If you have too many servants, they will only interfere with each other, and stand staring at the guests.

Give your orders before dinner, and through the meal never speak to the servants. Your whole attention must be given to the guests. Even if you see that matters are going wrong, do not let your annoyance appear, but gracefully ignore the painful facts. Let each servant have his regular position at the table. One should take the guests at the right of the hostess, and the left of the host; the other the guests on the other side. They should wear light, noiseless shoes, and white gloves, and each one carry a folded napkin over his right arm.

T HE main point in the arrangement of the table itself, is to secure beauty, without interfering with conversation. The table cover and napkins must be of snowy damask, the glass clear as crystal, and taste must preside over each detail. Let nothing high be placed on the table, that will effectually separate the guests from each other. There should be, first, a handsome centre piece, and this may be of glass, silver, or china, and not too high or large, and must be elegant as a work of art, or it is better omitted altogether. Preserve or fruit stands, tastefully decorated, with the fruit on fresh, green leaves, and flowers mingled with them, form exquisite centre pieces. A pyramid of flowers, or tasty vase or basket, forms, too, a beautiful ornament for the centre of the table. In addition to this, the French scatter vases of flowers all over the table, at the corners and in the centre. Some place a small, fragrant bouquet before the plate of each guest. Nothing can be more beautiful than this arrangement. Glasses of celery, dishes of clear, transparent jellies or preserves, exquisite little glass plates of pickles should stand in order on the table.

PLACE before each guest, the plate, knife, fork, spoon, four wine-glasses of various sizes, the goblet for water, napkin, small salt cellar, salt-spoon, and roll of bread. Place none of the meats or vegetables upon the large table. These should all be served at a side table, each guest selecting his own, to be handed by the servants. The first course is soup. As this is not meant to destroy the appetite for other viands, it should be light, not too rich or thick. Let the servant hand one ladleful to each person. If you have more than one kind, he must first enquire which each guest prefers.

IF you have wines, let them be handed round after the soup.

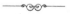

NEXT comes the fish. If you have large fish, let a slice, cut smoothly, not made into a hash by awkward carving, be placed upon the plate of the guest, with a slice of egg, and drawn butter. If the fish are small, one should be placed upon each plate.

THEN come the patties of oysters, minced veal, or lobster; or, instead of these, you may have poultry or game.

NEXT the roast. With the meats have vegetables served on a separate plate, that the guest may take as much as he wishes with meat. You will, of course, have a variety of vegetables, but scarcely any guest will choose more than two.

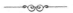

THE pastry and puddings come next in order, and these, too, are better served from a side table. Between the pastry and the dessert, have salad and cheese placed before each guest.

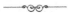

IF you eat dessert in the same room that you dine in, it should be placed upon the table (with the exception of the ices) before the guests are seated, and this comes after the pastry has been discussed. It should consist of fruit and ices.

A PLEASANTER and more elegant way, is to have the fruit and ices spread in a separate room, and leave the dining room after the pastry has been eaten. The change of position, the absence of the meat flavour in the atmosphere, make the dessert much more delightful than if it is eaten in the same room as the dinner. In summer especially, the change to a cool, fresh room, where the ices and fruits are tastefully spread, and flowers are scattered profusely about the room, delights every sense.

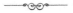

C OFFEE follows the dessert, and when this enters, if your guests are gentlemen only, your duty is at an end. You may then rise, leave the room, and need not reappear. If you have lady guests, you give the signal for rising after coffee, and lead the way to the parlour, where, in a few moments, the gentlemen will again join you.

S UPPOSE your guests invited, servants instructed, every arrangement made, and the important day arrived. The next point to consider is the reception of your guests. Be dressed in good season, as many seem to consider an invitation to dinner as one to pass the day, and come early. Take a position in your drawing room, where each guest will find you easily, and remain near it, until every guest has arrived. As each one enters, advance to meet him, and extend your hand.

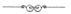

H AVE plenty of chairs ready in the drawing room, as an invitation to dinner by no means argues a 'stand up' party. As you have already arranged every detail, your duty as hostess consists in receiving your guests gracefully, conversing and looking as charmingly as possible. Flowers in the drawing room are as great a proof of taste as in the dining room.

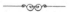

A s the time just before dinner is very apt to be tiresome, you should bring forward all the armour against stupidity that you possess. Display upon tables arranged conveniently about the room, curiosities, handsome books, photographs, engravings, stereoscopes, medallions, any works of art you may own, and have the ottomans, sofas, and chairs so placed that your guests can move easily about the room, or rooms.

T HE severest test of good breeding in a lady, is in the position of hostess, receiving dinner guests. Your guests may arrive all at once, yet you must make each one feel that he or she is the object of your individual attention, and none must be hurt by neglect. They may arrive very early, yet your duty is to make the time fly until dinner is announced. They may come late, and risk the ruin of your choicest dishes, yet you must not, upon pain of a breach of etiquette, show the least annoyance. If you know that the whole kitchen is in arms at the delay, you must conceal the anguish, as the Spartan boy did his pangs, to turn a cheerful, smiling face upon the tardy guests.

W HEN dinner is announced, you will lead the way to the dining room upon the arm of one of your gentlemen guests, having paired off the company in couples. The host comes in last with a lady upon his arm.

Y OU may indicate to each couple, as they enter the dining room, the seats they are to occupy, standing until all are seated, or you may allow them to choose their own places. The English fashion of placing a card upon each plate with the name of the person to take that seat upon it, is a good one. It enables the hostess to place those whom she is certain will be mutually entertaining, next each other. Place the gentleman who escorts you from the parlour at your right hand.

HAVING once taken your seat at table, you have nothing to do with the dinner but to partake of it. Not a word, or even a glance, will a well-bred hostess bestow upon the servants, nor will she speak to the guests of the dishes. Their choice rests between themselves and the waiters, and you must take no notice of what they eat, how much, or how little. Nay, should they partake of one dish only, you must ignore the fact.

THE greatest tact is displayed where the hostess makes each guest feel perfectly at ease. She will aid her husband both in leading and supporting the conversation, and will see that no guest is left in silence from want of attention. Whilst she ignores every breach of etiquette her guests may commit, she must carefully observe every rule herself, and this she must do in an easy, natural manner, avoiding every appearance of restraint.

TO watch the servants, or appear uneasy, lest something should go wrong, is excessively ill-bred, and if any accident does occur, you only make it worse by noticing it. To reprove or speak sharply to a servant before your guests, manifests a shocking want of good breeding.

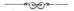

DINNER not being served from a side table, you must, while putting tasteful ornaments upon it, be careful not to crowd them, and leave room for the substantial dishes.

YOU must watch the plate of each guest, to see that it is well provided, and you will invite each one to partake of the various dishes.

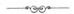

HAVE a servant to pass the plates from you to each guest, and from the host to you, after he has put the meat upon them, that you may add gravy and vegetables before they are set before your visitors.

AT these smaller dinner companies, avoid apologising for anything, either in the viands or the arrangement of them. You have provided the best your purse will allow, prepared as faultlessly as possible; you will only gain credit for mock modesty if you apologise for a well-prepared, well-spread dinner, and if there are faults they will only be made more conspicuous if attention is drawn to them by an apology.

EASE of manner, quiet dignity, cheerful, intelligent conversation, and gentle, ladylike deportment, never appear more charming than when they adorn a lady at the head of her own table.

CHAPTER XII

Dinner Company

ETIQUETTE FOR THE GUEST

W HEN you receive an invitation to join a dinner party, answer it immediately, as, by leaving your hostess in doubt whether you intend to accept or decline her hospitality, you make it impossible for her to decide how many she must prepare for. If you accept at first, and any unforeseen event keeps you from fulfilling your engagement, write a second note, that your hostess may not wait dinner for you. Such a note, if circumstances render it necessary to write it, may be sent with perfect propriety an hour before the time appointed for dinner, though, if you are aware that you cannot attend, earlier, you must send the information in good season.

Y OU should enter the house of your hostess from a quarter to half an hour earlier than the time appointed for dining. Proceed at once to the dressing room, and arrange your dress and hair, and then enter the drawing room. By going to the house too early, you may hasten or interrupt the toilet arrangements of your hostess; while, by being late, you will establish a most disagreeable association in the minds of all present, as 'the lady who kept dinner waiting at Mrs L—'s'.

IMMEDIATELY upon entering the parlour find your hostess, and speak to her first. It is very rude to stop to chat with other guests before greeting the lady of the house. You may bow to anyone you know, in passing, but do not stop to speak. Having exchanged a few words with your hostess, turn to the other guests, unless you are the first arrival. In that case, converse with your host and hostess until others come in.

BE careful, if dinner is delayed by the tardiness of the guests, or from any other cause, that you do not show by your manner that you are aware of such delay. To look towards the door often, consult your watch, or give tokens of weariness, are all marks of ill-breeding. Your hostess will probably be sufficiently annoyed by the irregularity itself; do not add to her discomfort by allowing her to suppose that her guests perceive the deficiencies. Look over the books and pictures with an air of interest, converse cheerfully, and in every way appear as if dinner were a matter of secondary importance (as, indeed, it should be) compared with the pleasure of the society around you.

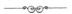

WHEN the signal for dinner is given, your hostess will probably name your escort to the table. If he is a stranger, bow in acknowledgement of the introduction, take his arm, and fall into your place in the stream of guests passing from the parlour to the dining room.

TAKE the seat pointed out by your hostess, or the waiter, as soon as it is offered. Each one will do this upon entering, and it prevents the confusion that will result if those first entering the room, remain standing until all the other guests come in.

WHEN you take your seat, be careful that your chair does not stand upon the dress of the lady next you, as she may not rise at the same instant that you do, and so you risk tearing her dress.

SIT gracefully at the table; neither so close as to make your movements awkward, nor so far away as to drag your food over your dress before it reaches your mouth. It is well to carry in your pocket a small pincushion, and, having unfolded your napkin, to pin it at the belt. You may do this quietly, without its being perceived, and you will thus really save your dress. If the napkin is merely laid open upon your lap, it will be very apt to slip down, if your dress is of silk or satin, and you risk the chance of appearing again in the drawing room with the front of your dress soiled or greased.

I F, by the carelessness or awkwardness of your neighbours or the servants, you have a plate of soup, glass of wine, or any dish intended for your mouth, deposited upon your dress, do not spring up, or make any exclamation. You may wipe off the worst of the spot with your napkin, and then let it pass without further notice. If an apology is made by the unlucky perpetrator of the accident, try to set him at his ease by your own ladylike composure. He will feel sorry and awkward enough, without reproach, sullenness, or cold looks from you.

G LOVES and mittens are no longer worn at table, even at the largest dinner parties.

T O make remarks upon the guests or the dishes is excessively rude.

I F the conversation is general, speak loudly enough to be heard by those around you, but, at the same time, avoid raising your voice *too* much. If the company is very large, and you converse only with the person immediately beside you, speak in a distinct, but low tone, that you may not interrupt other couples, but carefully avoid whispering or a confidential air. Both are in excessively bad taste. To laugh in a suppressed way, has the appearance of laughing at those around you, and a loud, boisterous laugh is always unladylike. Converse cheerfully, laugh quietly, but freely, if you will, and while you confine your attention entirely to your neighbour, still avoid any air of secrecy or mystery.

Never use an eyeglass, either to look at the persons around you or the articles upon the table.

Eat your soup quietly. To make any noise in eating it, is simply disgusting. Do not break bread into your soup. Break off small pieces and put into your mouth, if you will, but neither bite it from the roll nor break it up, and eat it from your soup-plate with a spoon.

In eating bread with meat, never dip it into the gravy on your plate, and then bite the end off. If you wish to eat it with gravy, break off a small piece, put it upon your plate, and then, with a fork, convey it to your mouth.

When helped to fish, remove, with knife and fork, all the bones, then lay down the knife, and, with a piece of bread in your left hand and a fork in your right, eat the flakes of fish.

NEED I say that the knife is to cut your food with, and must never be used while eating? To put it in your mouth is a distinctive mark of low-breeding.

IF you have selected what you will eat, keep the plate that is placed before you; never pass it to the persons next you, as they may have an entirely different choice of meat or vegetables.

NEVER attempt to touch any dish that is upon the table, but out of your reach, by stretching out your arms, leaning forward, or, still worse, standing up. Ask the waiter to hand it, if you wish for it; or, if the gentleman beside you can easily do so, you may ask him to pass it to you.

DO not press those near you to take more or other things than are upon their plate. This is the duty of the hostess, or, if the company is large, the servants will attend to it. For you to do so is officious and ill-bred.

WHEN conversing let your knife and fork rest easily upon your plate, even if still in your hand. Avoid holding them upright. Keep your own knife, fork, and spoon solely for the articles upon your own plate. To use them for helping yourself to butter or salt, is rude in the extreme.

WHEN you do not use the salt-spoon, sugar-tongs, and butter-knife, you may be sure that those around you will conclude that you have never seen the articles, and do not know their use.

YOU need not fear to offend by refusing to take wine with a gentleman, even your host. If you decline gracefully, he will appreciate the delicacy which makes you refuse. If, however, you have no conscientious scruples, and are invited to take wine, bow, and merely raise the glass to your lips, then set it down again. You may thus acknowledge the courtesy, and yet avoid actually drinking the wine.

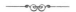

NO lady should drink wine at dinner. Even if her head is strong enough to bear it, she will find her cheeks, soon after the indulgence, flushed, hot, and uncomfortable; and if the room is warm, and the dinner a long one, she will probably pay the penalty of her folly, by having a headache all the evening.

IF offered any dish of which you do not wish to partake, decline it, but do not assign any reason. To object to the dish itself is an insult to your entertainers, and if you assert any reason for your own dislike it is ill-bred.

D O not bend too much forward over your food, and converse easily. To eat fast, or appear to be so much engrossed as to be unable to converse, is ill-bred; and it makes those around you suspect that you are so little accustomed to dining well, that you fear to stop eating an instant, lest you should not get enough.

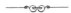

I T is equally ill-bred to accept everything that is offered to you. Never take more than two vegetables; do not take a second plate of soup, pastry, or pudding. Indeed, it is best to accept but *one* plate of any article.

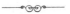

N EVER use a spoon for anything but liquids, and never touch anything to eat, excepting bread, celery, or fruit, with your fingers.

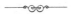

I N the intervals which must occur between the courses, do not appear to be conscious of the lapse of time. Wear a careless air when waiting, conversing cheerfully and pleasantly, and avoid looking round the room, as if wondering what the waiters are about.

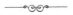

N EVER eat every morsel that is upon your plate; and surely no lady will ever scrape her plate, or pass the bread round it, as if to save the servants the trouble of washing it.

—⁂—

TAKE such small mouthfuls that you can always be ready for conversation, but avoid playing with your food, or partaking of it with an affectation of delicate appetite. Your hostess may suppose you despise her fare, if you appear so very choice, or eat too sparingly. If your state of health deprives you of appetite, it is bad enough for you to decline the invitation to dine out.

—⁂—

NEVER examine minutely the food before you. You insult your hostess by such a proceeding, as it looks as if you feared to find something upon the plate that should not be there.

—⁂—

IF you find a worm on opening a nut, or in any of the fruit, hand your plate quietly, and without remark, to the waiter, and request him to bring you a clean one. Do not let others perceive the movement, or the cause of it, if you can avoid so doing.

—⁂—

NEVER make a noise in eating. To munch or smack the lips are vulgar faults.

—⁂—

SIT quietly at table, avoid stiffness, but, at the same time, be careful that you do not annoy others by your restlessness.

D o not eat so fast as to be done long before others, nor so slowly as to keep them waiting.

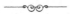

W hen the finger-glasses are passed round, dip the ends of your fingers into them, and wipe them upon your napkin; then do not fold your napkin, but place it beside your plate upon the table.

T o carry away fruit or bonbons from the table is a sign of low breeding.

R ise with the other ladies when your hostess gives the signal.

A fter returning to the parlour, remain in the house at least an hour after dinner is over. If you have another engagement in the evening, you may then take your leave, but not before. You will insult your hostess by leaving sooner, as it appears that you came only for the dinner, and that being over, your interest in the house, for the time, has ceased. It is only beggars who 'eat and run!'

CHAPTER XIII

———◦⊙◦———

Table Etiquette

I N order to appear perfectly well bred at table when in
company, or in public, as at a hotel, you must pay attention,
three times a day, to the points of table etiquette. If you
neglect these little details at home and in private, they will be
performed awkwardly and with an air of restraint when you
are in company. By making them habitual, they will become
natural, and appear easily, and sit gracefully upon you.

———◦⊙◦———

E VEN when eating entirely alone, observe these little details,
thus making the most finished and elegant manners
perfectly familiar, and thus avoiding the stiff, awkward air you
will wear if you keep your politeness only for company, when
you will be constantly apprehensive of doing wrong.

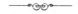

———◦⊙◦———

A T breakfast or tea, if your seat is at the head of the table,
you must, before taking anything upon your own plate,
fill a cup for each one of the family, and pass them round,
being careful to suit each one in the preparation of the cup,
that none may return to you for more tea, water, sugar, or

milk. If you have a visitor, pass the cup with the tea or coffee alone in it, and hand with the cup the sugar bowl and cream pitcher, that these may be added in the quantity preferred.

AFTER all the cups have been filled and passed round, you may take the bread, butter, and other food upon your own plate. Train your children, so that they will pass these things to you as soon as they see you are ready to receive them.

IF you are yourself at the side of the table, pass the bread, butter, etc., to the lady at the head, when you see that she has sent the cups from the waiter before her, to those seated at the table.

IF you occupy the place of head of the table, you must watch the cups, offer to fill them when empty, and also see that each one of the family is well helped to the other articles upon the table.

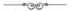

AVOID making any noise in eating, even if each meal is eaten in solitary state. It is a disgusting habit, and one not easily cured if once contracted, to make any noise with the lips when eating.

NEVER put large pieces of food into your mouth. Eat slowly, and cut your food into small pieces before putting it into your mouth.

USE your fork, or spoon, never your knife, to put your food into your mouth. At dinner, hold in your left hand a piece of bread, and raise your meat or vegetables with the fork, holding the bread to prevent the pieces slipping from the plate.

IF you are asked at table what part of the meat you prefer, name your favourite piece, but do not give such information unless asked to do so. To point out any especial part of a dish, and ask for it, is ill-bred. To answer, when asked to select a part, that 'it is a matter of indifference', or, 'I can eat any part', is annoying to the carver, as he cares less than yourself certainly, and would prefer to give you the piece you really like best.

DO not pour coffee or tea from your cup into your saucer, and do not blow either these or soup. Wait until they cool.

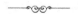

USE the butter-knife, salt-spoon, and sugar-tongs as scrupulously when alone, as if a room full of people were watching you. Otherwise, you may neglect to do so when the omission will mortify you.

Never put poultry or fish bones, or the stones of fruit, upon the tablecloth, but place them on the edge of your plate.

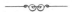

Do not begin to eat until others at the table are ready to commence too.

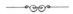

Sit easily in your chair, neither too near the table, nor too far from it, and avoid such tricks as putting your arms on the table, leaning back lazily in your chair, or playing with your knife, fork, or spoon.

Never pass your plate with the knife or fork upon it, and when you pass your cup, put the spoon in the saucer.

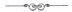

Never pile up the food on your plate. It looks as if you feared it would all be gone before you could be helped again, and it will certainly make your attempts to cut the food awkward, if your plate is crowded.

IF there is a delicacy upon the table, partake of it sparingly, and never help yourself to it a second time.

IF you wish to cough, or use your handkerchief, rise from the table, and leave the room. If you have not time to do this, cover your mouth, and turn your head aside from the table, and perform the disagreeable necessity as rapidly and quietly as possible.

AVOID gesticulation at the table. Indeed, a well-bred lady will never gesticulate, but converse quietly, letting the expression and animation of her features give force to her words.

NEVER, when at the home table, leave it until the other members of the family are also ready to rise.

CHAPTER XIV

—◦⟨⟩◦—

Conduct in the Street

A LADY'S conduct is never so entirely at the mercy of critics, because never so public, as when she is in the street. Her dress, carriage, walk, will all be exposed to notice; every passer-by will look at her, if it is only for one glance; every unladylike action will be marked; and in no position will a dignified, ladylike deportment be more certain to command respect.

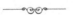

L ET me start with you upon your promenade, my friend, and I will soon decide your place upon the list of well-bred ladies.

F IRST, your dress. Not that scarlet shawl, with a green dress, I beg, and – oh! spare my nerves! – you are not so insane as to put on a blue bonnet. That's right. If you wish to wear the green dress, don a black shawl, and – that white bonnet will do very well. One rule you must lay down with regard to a walking dress. It must never be conspicuous. Let the material be rich, if you will; the set of each garment faultless; have collar and sleeves snowy white, and wear neatly-fitting, whole, clean gloves and boots. Every detail may be scrupulously attended to, but let the whole effect be quiet and modest. Wear a little of one bright colour, if you will, but not more than one. Let each part of the dress harmonise with all the rest; avoid the *extreme* of fashion, and let the dress suit *you.* If you are short and plump, do not wear flounces, because they are fashionable, and avoid large plaids, even if they are the very latest style. If tall and slight, do not add to the length of your figure by long stripes, a little mantilla, and a caricature of a bonnet, with long, streaming ribbons. A large, round face will never look well, staring from a tiny, delicate bonnet; nor will a long, thin one stand the test much better. Wear what is becoming to *yourself,* and only bow to fashion enough to avoid eccentricity. To have everything in the *extreme* of fashion, is a sure mark of vulgarity.

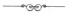

WEAR no jewellery in the street excepting your watch and brooch. Jewellery is only suited for full evening dress, when all the other details unite to set it off. If it is real, it is too valuable to risk losing in the street, and if it is *not* real, no lady should wear it. Mock jewellery is utterly detestable.

WHAT are you doing? Sucking the head of your parasol! Have you not breakfasted? Take that piece of ivory from your mouth! To suck it is unladylike, and let me tell you, excessively unbecoming. Rosy lips and pearly teeth can be put to a better use.

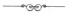

WHY did you not dress before you came out? It is a mark of ill-breeding to draw your gloves on in the street. Now your bonnet-strings, and now – your collar! Pray arrange your dress before you leave the house! Nothing looks worse than to see a lady fussing over her dress in the street. Take a few moments more in your dressing room, and so arrange your dress that you will not need to think of it again whilst you are out.

DO not walk so fast! you are not chasing anybody! Walk slowly, gracefully! Oh, do not drag one foot after the other as if you were fast asleep – set down the foot lightly, but at the same time firmly; now, carry your head up, not so; you hang it down as if you feared to look anyone in the face! Nay, that is the other extreme! Now you look like a drill-major, on parade! So! that is the medium. Erect, yet, at the same time, easy and elegant.

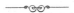

NOW, my friend, do not swing your arms. You don't know what to do with them? Your parasol takes one hand; hold your dress up a little with the other. Not so! No lady should raise her dress above the ankle.

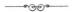

TAKE care! don't drag your dress through that mud-puddle! Worse and worse! If you take hold of your dress on both sides, in that way, and drag it up so high, you will be set down as a raw country girl. So. Raise it just above the boot, all round, easily, letting it fall again in the old folds. Don't shake it down; it will fall back of itself.

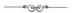

S TOP! don't you see there is a carriage coming? Do you want to be thrown down by the horses? You can run across? Very ladylike indeed! Surely nothing can be more ungraceful than to see a lady shuffle and run across a street. Wait until the way is clear and then walk slowly across.

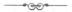

D O not try to raise your skirts. It is better to soil them. (You were very foolish to wear white skirts this muddy day.) *They* are easily washed, and you cannot raise *all*. You will surely be awkward in making the attempt, and probably fail, in spite of your efforts. True, they will be badly soiled, and you expose this when you raise the dress, but the state of the streets must be seen by all who see your share of the dirt, and they will apologise for your untidy appearance in a language distinctly understood.

D ON'T hold your parasol so close to your face, nor so low down. You cannot see your way clear, and you will run against somebody. Always hold an umbrella or parasol so that it will clear your bonnet, and leave the space before your face open, that you may see your way clearly.

I F you are ever caught in a shower, and meet a gentleman friend who offers an umbrella, accept it, if he will accompany you to your destination; but do not deprive him of it, if he is not able to join you. Should he insist, return it to his house or store the instant you reach home, with a note of thanks. If a stranger offers you the same services, decline it positively, but courteously, at the same time thanking him.

N EVER stop to speak to a gentleman in the street. If you have anything important to say to him, allow him to join and walk with you, but do not stop. It is best to follow the same rule with regard to ladies, and either walk with them or invite them to walk with you, instead of stopping to talk.

A LADY who desires to pay strict regard to etiquette, will not stop to gaze in at the shop windows. It looks countrified. If she is alone, it looks as if she were waiting for someone; and if she is not alone, she is victimising someone else, to satisfy her curiosity.

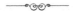

R EMEMBER that in meeting your gentlemen friends it is your duty to speak first, therefore do not cut them by waiting to be recognised. Be sure, however, that they see you before you bow, or you place yourself in the awkward position of having your bow pass, unreturned.

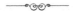

YOU are not expected to recognise any friend on the opposite side of the street. Even if you see them, do not bow.

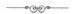

AVOID 'cutting' anyone. It is a small way of showing spite, and lowers you more than your enemy. If you wish to avoid any further intercourse bow, coldly and gravely, but do not look at anyone, to whom you are in the habit of bowing, and pass without bowing. If you do this, they may flatter themselves that they were really unrecognised, but a distant, cold bow will show them that you speak from civility only, not from friendship.

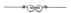

IN the street a lady takes the arm of a relative, her affianced lover, or husband, but of no other gentleman, unless the streets are slippery, or in the evening.

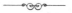

WHEN a lady walks with two gentlemen, she should endeavour to divide her attention and remarks equally between them.

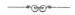

IF you do stop in the street, draw near the walls, that you may not keep others from passing.

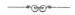

L OUD talking and laughing in the street are excessively vulgar. Not only this, but they expose a lady to the most severe misconstruction. Let your conduct be modest and quiet.

I F a gentleman, although a stranger, offers his hand to assist you in leaving a carriage, omnibus, or to aid you in crossing where it is wet or muddy, accept his civility, thank him, bow and pass on.

I F you wish to take an omnibus or car, see that it is not already full. If it is, do not get in. You will annoy others, and be uncomfortable yourself.

CHAPTER XV

———✿———

Letter Writing

THERE is no branch of education called so universally into requisition as the art of letter writing; no station, high or low, where the necessity for correspondence is not felt; no person, young or old, who does not, at some time, write, cause to be written, and receive letters. From the President in his official capacity, with the busy pens of secretaries constantly employed in this branch of service, to the Irish labourer who, unable to guide a pen, writes, also by proxy, to his kinsfolks across the wide ocean; all, at some time, feel the desire to transmit some message, word of love, business, or sometimes enmity, by letter.

———✿———

YET, in spite of the universal need, and almost universal habit, there are really but very few persons who write a *good* letter; a letter that is, at the same time long enough to interest, yet not long enough to tire; sufficiently condensed to keep the attention, and not tedious, and yet detailed enough to afford satisfaction; that is correct in grammatical construction, properly punctuated, written in a clear, legible hand, with the date, address, signature, all in the proper place, no words whose letters stand in utter defiance to spelling-book rules; in short, a well-written letter.

THOUSANDS, millions are sent from post to post every day. The lightning speed of the telegraph takes its messages from city to city; the panting steamer carries from continent to continent its heavy mail-bags, laden with its weight of loving messages; the 'iron horse' drags behind it, its measure of the many missives; while, in the far-distant Western wilds, the lumbering wagon bears its paper freight, with its pen eloquence, to cheer and comfort, or sadden and crush, the waiting emigrants, longing for news of home.

TO some, who, with hearts desolated by the separation from the home circle, could read, with an eager interest, volumes of the most commonplace, trivial incidents, if only connected with the loved ones there, will come pages, from the pen of the dearest relative, full of learning, wit, and wisdom, wholly uninteresting to the receiver.

WHY is this? Not from any desire upon the part of the writer to display learning or talent, but because, writing a letter being to them a great undertaking, and the letter being destined to go a long distance, they look upon it as an event too unusual to be wasted in detailing the simple, everyday details of domestic life, and ransack memory and learning for a subject worthy of the long journey and unusual labour.

O THERS will have, from mere acquaintances, long, tedious details of uninteresting trivialities, and from the near relatives, short, dry epistles, which fall like stones upon the heart longing for little, affectionate expressions, and home memories.

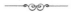

F ROM some letter writers, who are in the midst of scenes and events of the most absorbing interest, letters arrive, only a few lines long, without one allusion to the interesting matter lying so profusely around them; while others, with the scantiest of outward subjects, will, from their own teeming brain, write bewitching, absorbing epistles, read with eagerness, laid aside with the echo of Oliver Twist's petition in a sigh; the reader longing for 'more'.

I T is, of course, impossible to lay down any distinct rule for the *style* of letter writing. Embracing, as it does, all subjects and all classes, all countries and associations, and every relation in which one person can stand to another, what would be an imperative rule in some cases, becomes positive absurdity in others. Every letter will vary from others written before, in either its subject, the person addressed, or the circumstances which make it necessary to write it.

L ETTER writing is, in fact, but conversation, carried on with the pen, when distance or circumstances prevent the easier method of exchanging ideas, by spoken words. Write, therefore, as you would speak, were the person to whom your letter is addressed seated beside you. As amongst relatives and intimate friends you would converse with a familiar manner, and in easy language, so in your letters to such persons, let your style be simple, entirely devoid of effort.

AGAIN, when introduced to a stranger, or conversing with one much older than yourself, your manner is respectful and dignified; so let the letters addressed to those on these terms with yourself, be written in a more ceremonious style, but at the same time avoid stiffness, and above all, pedantry. A letter of advice to a child, would of course demand an entirely different style, from that written by a young lady to a friend or relative advanced in life; yet the general rule, 'write as you would converse', applies to each and every case.

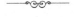

NEATNESS is an important requisite in a letter. To send a fair, clean sheet, with the words written in a clear, legible hand, will go a great way in ensuring a cordial welcome for your letter. Avoid erasures, as they spoil the beauty of your sheet. If it is necessary to correct a word, draw your pen through it, and write the word you wish to use as a substitute, above the one erased; do not scratch out the word and write another over it: it is untidy, and the second word is seldom legible. Another requisite for a good letter is a clear, concise style. Use language that will be easily understood, and avoid the parenthesis. Important passages in letters are often lost entirely, by the ambiguous manner in which they are worded, or rendered quite as unintelligible by the blots, erasures, or villainously bad handwriting. A phrase may, by the addition or omission of one word, or by the alteration of one punctuation mark, convey to the reader an entirely different idea from that intended by the writer; so, while you write plainly, use good language, you must also write carefully, and punctuate properly.

I F you are in doubt about the correct spelling of a word, do not trust to chance, hoping it may be right, but get a dictionary, and be certain that you have spelt it as it ought to be.

S IMPLICITY is a great charm in letter-writing. What you send in a letter, is, as a general rule, intended for the perusal of one person only. Therefore to cumber your epistles with quotations, similes, flowery language, and a stilted, pedantic style, is in bad taste. You may use elegant language, yet use it easily. If you use a quotation, let it come into its place naturally, as if flowing in perfect harmony with your ideas, and let it be short. Long quotations in a letter are tiresome. Make no attempt at display in a correspondence. You will err as much in such an attempt, as if, when seated face to face with your correspondent, alone in your own apartment, you were to rise and converse with the gestures and language of a minister in his pulpit, or a lecturer upon his platform.

A s everything, in style, depends upon the subject of the letter, and the person to whom it is addressed, some words follow, relating to some of the various kinds of correspondence:

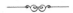

B USINESS LETTERS should be as brief as is consistent with the subject; clear, and to the point. Say all that is necessary, in plain, distinct language, and say no more. State, in forcible words, every point that it is desirable for your correspondent to be made acquainted with, that your designs and prospects upon the subject may be perfectly well understood. Write, in such a letter, of nothing but the business in hand; other matters will be out of place there. Nowhere is a confused style, or illegible writing, more unpardonable than in a business letter; nowhere a good style and hand more important. Avoid flowery language, too many words, all pathos or wit, any display of talent or learning, and every merely personal matter, in a business letter.

L ETTERS OF CONGRATULATION demand a cheerful, pleasant style, and an appearance of great interest. They should be written from the heart, and the cordial, warm feelings there will prompt the proper language. Be careful, while offering to your friend the hearty congratulations her happy circumstances demand, that you do not let envy at her good fortune, creep into your head, to make the pen utter complaining words at your own hard lot. Do not dampen her joy, by comparing her happiness with the misery of another. There are many clouds in the life of every one of us. While the sun shines clearly upon the events of your friend's life let her enjoy the brightness and warmth, unshadowed by any words of yours. Give her, to the full, your sympathy in her rejoicing, cheerful words, warm congratulations, and bright hopes for the future. Should there be, at the time of her happiness, any sad event you wish to communicate to her, of which it is your duty to inform her, write it in another letter. If you must send it the same day, do so, but let the epistle wishing her joy, go alone, unclouded with the news of sorrow. At the same time, avoid exaggerated expressions of congratulation, lest you are suspected of a desire to be satirical, and avoid underlining any words. If the language is not forcible enough to convey your ideas, you will not make it better by underlining it. If you say to your friend upon her marriage, that you wish her '*joy* in her new relations, and *hope* she may be *entirely happy* in her domestic life', you make her doubt your wishes, and think you mean to ridicule her chances of such happiness.

L ETTERS OF CONDOLENCE are exceedingly trying, both to read and to write. If the affliction which calls for them is one which touches you nearly, really grieving and distressing you, all written words must seem tame and cold, compared with the aching sympathy which dictates them. It is hard with the eyes blinded by tears, and the hand shaking, to write calmly; and it is impossible to express upon paper all the burning thoughts and words that would pour forth, were you beside the friend whose sorrow is yours. If you do not feel the trial, your task is still more difficult, for no letters demand truth, spoken from the heart, more than letters of condolence. Do not treat the subject for grief too lightly. Write words of comfort if you will, but do not appear to consider the affliction as a trifle. Time may make it less severe, but the first blow of grief must be heavy, and a few words of sincere sympathy will outweigh pages of mere expressions of hope for comfort, or the careless lines that show the letter to be one of mere duty, not feeling. Let your friend feel that her sorrow makes her dearer to you than ever before, and that her grief is yours. To treat the subject with levity, or to wander from it into witticisms or everyday chit-chat, is a wanton insult, unworthy of a lady and a friend. Do not magnify the event, or plunge the mourner into still deeper despondency by taking a despairing, gloomy view of the sorrow, under which she is bent. Show her the silver lining of her cloud, try to soothe her grief, yet be willing to admit that it *is* a cloud, and that she *has* cause for grief. To throw out hints that the sorrow is sent as a punishment to an offender; to imply that neglect or imprudence on the part of the mourner is the cause of the calamity; to hold up the trial as an example of retribution, or a natural consequence of wrong doing, is cruel, and barbarous. Even if this is true (indeed, if this is the case, it only aggravates the insult); avoid such retrospection. It is as if a surgeon, called in to a patient suffering from a fractured limb, sat down, inattentive to the suffering, to lecture his patient upon the carelessness which caused the accident. One of the most touching letters of condolence ever written was sent by a literary lady, well known in the ranks of our American authoresses, to her sister, who had lost her youngest child. The words were few, merely:

Sister Darling:

I cannot write what is in my heart for you today, it is too full. Filled with a double sorrow; for you, for my own grief. Tears blind me, my pen trembles in my hand. Oh, to be near you! to clasp you in my arms! to draw your head to my bosom, and weep with you! Darling, God comfort you, I cannot.

S.

T HAT was all. Yet the sorrowing mother said that no other letter, though she appreciated the kind motive that dictated all, yet none comforted her as did these few lines. Written from the heart, their simple eloquence touched the heart for which they were intended. Early stages of great grief reject *comfort*, but they long, with intense longing, for sympathy.

L ETTERS WRITTEN TO GENTLEMEN should be ceremonious and dignified. If the acquaintance is slight, write in the third person, if there is a necessity for a letter. If a business letter, be respectful, yet not servile. It is better to avoid correspondence with gentlemen, particularly whilst you are young, as there are many objections to it. Still, if a friend of long standing solicits a correspondence, and your parents or husband approve and permit compliance with the request, it would be over-prudish to refuse. Write, however, such letters as, if they were printed in the newspapers, would cause you no annoyance. If the acquaintance admits of a frank, friendly style, be careful that your expressions of goodwill do not become too vehement, and avoid any confidential communications. When he begins to ask you to keep such and such passages secret, believe me, it is quite time to drop the correspondence.

Letters of Thanks for enquiries made, should be short, merely echoing the words of the letter they answer, and contain the answer to the question, with an acknowledgement of your correspondent's interest. If the letter is your own acknowledgement of a favour conferred, let the language be simple, but strong, grateful, and graceful. Fancy that you are clasping the hand of the kind friend who has been generous or thoughtful for you, and then write, even as you would speak. Never hint that you deem such a favour an obligation to be returned at the first opportunity; although this may really be the case, it is extremely indelicate to say so. In your letter gracefully acknowledge the obligation, and if, at a later day, you can return the favour, then let actions, not words, prove your grateful recollection of the favour conferred upon you. If your letter is written to acknowledge the reception of a present, speak of the beauty or usefulness of the gift, and of the pleasant associations with her name it will always recall.

Letters of Recommendation should be truthful, polite, and carefully considered. Such letters may be business letters, or they may be given to servants, and they must be given only when really deserved. Do not be hasty in giving them; remember that you are in some measure responsible for the bearer; therefore, never sacrifice truth and frankness, to a mistaken idea of kindness or politeness.

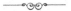

Letters of Introduction must be left unsealed. They must not contain any allusion to the personal qualities of the bearer, as such allusion would be about as sure a proof

of ill-breeding as if you sat beside your friend, and ran over
the list of the virtues and talents possessed by her. The fact
that the person bearing the letter is your friend, will be all
sufficient reason for cordial reception by the friend to whom
the letter is addressed. The best form is:

Philadelphia, June 18th, 18 –.

My Dear Mary:

*This letter will be handed to you by Mrs C., to whom I
am pleased to introduce you, certain that the acquaintance
thus formed, between two friends of mine, of so long standing
and so much beloved, will be pleasant to both parties. Any
attention that you may find it in your power to extend to Mrs
C. whilst she is in your city, will be highly appreciated, and
gratefully acknowledged, by*

*Your sincere friend
A–.*

L ETTERS OF EXCUSE should be frank and graceful. They
must be written promptly, as soon as the occasion that
calls for them admits. If delayed, they become insulting. If
such a letter is called forth by an act of negligence on your
own part, apologise for it frankly, and show by your tone that
you sincerely desire to regain the confidence your carelessness
has periled. If you have been obliged by positive inability to
neglect the fulfilment of any promise you have given, or any
commission you have undertaken, then state the reason for
your delay, and solicit the indulgence of your friend. Do not
write in such stiff, formal language that the apology will seem
forced from you, but offer your excuse frankly, as if with a

sincere desire to atone for an act of negligence, or remove a ground of offence.

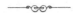

INVITATIONS are generally written in the third person, and this form is used where the acquaintance is very slight, for formal notes, and cards of compliment. The form is proper upon such occasions, but should be used only in the most ceremonious correspondence. If this style is adopted by a person who has been accustomed to write in a more familiar one to you, take it as a hint, that the correspondence has, for some reason, become disagreeable, and had better cease.

AUTOGRAPH LETTERS should be very short; merely acknowledging the compliment paid by the request for the signature, and a few words expressing the pleasure you feel in granting the favour. If you write to ask for an autograph, always enclose a postage stamp for the answer.

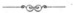

DATE every letter you write accurately, and avoid postscripts.

POLITENESS, kindness, both demand that every letter you receive must be answered. Nothing can give more pleasure in a correspondence, than prompt replies. Matters of much importance often rest upon the reply to a letter, and therefore this duty should never be delayed. In answering friendly letters, it will be found much easier to write what is kind and interesting, if you sit down to the task as soon as you read your friend's letter. Always mention the date of the letter to which your own is a reply.

Never write on a half sheet of paper. Paper is cheap, and a *half* sheet looks both mean and slovenly. If you do not write but three lines, still send the whole sheet of paper. Perfectly plain paper, thick, smooth, and white, is the most elegant. When in mourning, use paper and envelopes with a black edge. Never use the gilt edged, or fancy bordered paper; it looks vulgar, and is in bad taste. You may, if you will, have your initials stamped at the top of the sheet, and on the seal of the envelope, but do not have any fancy ornaments in the corners, or on the back of the envelope.

You will be guilty of a great breach of politeness, if you answer either a note or letter upon the half sheet of the paper sent by your correspondent, even though it may be left blank.

Never write, even the shortest note, in pencil. It looks careless, and is rude.

NEVER write a letter carelessly. It may be addressed to your most intimate friend, or your nearest relative, but you can never be sure that the eye for which it is intended, will be the *only* one that sees it. I do not mean by this, that the epistle should be in a formal, studied *style*, but that it must be correct in its grammatical construction, properly punctuated, with every word spelt according to rule. Even in the most familiar epistles, observe the proper rules for composition; you would not in conversing, even with your own family, use incorrect grammar, or impertinent language; therefore avoid saying upon paper what you would not say with your tongue.

NOTES written in the third person, must be continued throughout in the same person; they are frequently very mysterious from the confusion of pronouns, yet it is a style of correspondence much used and very proper upon many occasions. For compliment, enquiry where there is no intimacy between the parties, from superiors to inferiors, the form is elegant and proper. If you receive a note written in the third person, reply in the same form, but do not reply thus to a more familiar note or letter, as it is insulting, and implies offence taken. If you wish to repel undue familiarity or impertinence in your correspondent, then reply to the epistle in the most formal language, and in the third person.

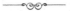

IT is an extraordinary fact, that persons who have received a good education, and who use their pens frequently, will often, in writing notes, commence in the third person and then use the second or first personal pronoun, and finish by a signature; thus –

> *Miss Claire's compliments to Mr James, and wishes to know whether you have finished reading my copy of 'Jane Eyre,' as if Mr James had finished it, I would like to lend it to another friend.*
>
> > *Sincerely yours,*
> > *Ella Claire.*

———◦❦◦———

T HE errors in the above are too glaring to need comment, yet, with only the alteration of names, it is a copy, *verbatim*, of a note written by a well-educated girl.

———◦❦◦———

N EVER sign a note written in the third person, if you begin the note with your own name. It is admissible, if the note is worded in this way:

> *Will Mr James return by bearer, the copy of 'Jane Eyre' he borrowed, if he has finished reading it, and oblige his sincere friend,*
>
> > *Ella Claire.*

———◦❦◦———

I F you use a quotation, never omit to put it in quotation marks, otherwise your correspondent may, however unjustly, accuse you of a desire to pass off the idea and words of another, for your own.

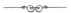

AVOID postscripts. Above all, never send an enquiry or compliment in a postscript. To write a long letter, upon various subjects, and in the postscript desire to be remembered to your friend's family, or enquire for their welfare, instead of a compliment, becomes insulting. It is better, if you have not time to write again and place such enquiries above your signature, to omit them entirely. Nobody likes to see their name mentioned as an afterthought.

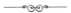

PUNCTUATE your letters carefully. The want of a mark of punctuation, or the incorrect placing of it, will make the most woeful confusion. I give an instance of the utter absurdity produced by the alteration of punctuation marks, turning a sensible paragraph to the most arrant nonsense:

'Cæsar entered; on his head his helmet; on his feet armed sandals; upon his brow there was a cloud; in his right hand his faithful sword; in his eye an angry glare; saying nothing, he sat down.'

BY using precisely the same words, merely altering the position of the punctuation marks, we have:

'Cæsar entered on his head; his helmet on his feet; armed sandals upon his brow; there was a cloud in his right hand; his faithful sword in his eye; an angry glare saying nothing; he sat down.'

B E careful, then, to punctuate properly, that you may convey to the reader the exact sense of what is in your mind.

I F you receive an impertinent letter, treat it with contempt; do not answer it.

N EVER answer a letter by proxy, when you are able to write yourself. It is a mark of respect and love, to answer, in your own hand, all letters addressed to you. If you are obliged to write to a friend to refuse to grant a favour asked, you will lessen the pain of refusal by wording your letter delicately. Loving words, if it is a near friend, respectful, kind ones if a mere acquaintance, will make the disagreeable contents of the letter more bearable. Try to make the *manner* smooth and soften the hardness of the *matter*.

E VERY letter must embrace the following particulars: 1st. The date. 2nd. The complimentary address. 3rd. The body of the letter. 4th. The complimentary closing. 5th. The signature. 6th. The address.

T HERE are two ways of putting the date, and the address. The first is to place them at the top of the sheet, the other is to place them after the signature.

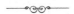

W HEN at the top, you write the name of your residence, or that of the city in which you reside, with the day of the month and the year, at the right hand of the first line of the sheet. Then, at the left hand of the next line, write the address, then the complimentary address below the name; thus –

Willow Grove, New York,
June 27th, 1859.

Mrs E. C. Howell,

My dear Madam,

I received your letter, etc.

At the end of the letter, on the right hand of the sheet, put the complimentary closing, and then the signature; thus –

I remain, my dear Madam,
With much respect,
Yours sincerely,
S. E. Law.

I F you place the date and address after the signature, put it at the left of the sheet; thus –

I remain, my dear Madam,
With much respect,
Yours sincerely,
S. E. Law.

Mrs E. C. Howell.
June 27th, 1859.

F OR a long letter, it is better to put the date and address at the top of the page. For a letter of only a few lines, which ends on the first page, the second form is best. In a letter written to a person in the same city, you need not put the address under the signature; if not, write it –

S. E. Law,
Willow Grove, New York.

I N writing to a dear friend or relative, where there is no formality required, you may omit the name at the top of the letter; put the date and address thus –

Willow Grove, New York,
June 27th, 1859.

Dear Anna:
I write, etc.
It is best, however, to put the full name at the bottom of the last page, in case the letter is mislaid without the envelope; thus –
E. C. Law.
Miss Anna Wright.

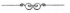

I F you use an envelope, and this custom is now universal, fold your letter neatly to fit into it; then direct on the envelope. Put first the name, then the name of the person to whose care the letter must be directed, then the street, the city, and State. If the town is small, put also the county.

T HIS is the form:

> Miss Anna Wright,
> Care of Mr John C. Wright,
> No. 40, Lexington street,
> Greensburg - Lee County.
> Mass.

O N the upper right hand corner of your envelope, put your postage-stamp.

I F you send a letter by private hand, write the name of the bearer in the lower left hand corner, thus:

> Mrs E. A. Howell,
> Clinton Place,
> Boston.

> Mr G. G. Lane.

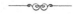

I N directing to anyone who can claim any prefix, or addition, to his proper name do not omit to put that 'republican title'.

F OR a clergyman, Rev. for Reverend is put before the name, thus –

Rev. James C. Day.

For a bishop:

Right Reverend E. Banks.

For a physician:

Dr James Curtis.

or,

James Curtis, M.D.

For a member of Congress:

Hon. E.C. Delta.

For an officer in the navy:

Capt. Henry Lee, U.S.N.

For an officer in the army:

Col. Edward Holmes, U. S. A.

For a professor:

Prof. E. L. James.

———◦◦◦———

I F you seal with wax, it is best to put a drop under the turn-over, and fasten this down firmly before you drop the wax that is to receive the impression.

———◦◦◦———

C ARDS of compliment are usually written in the third person. I give a few of the most common and proper forms.

F OR a party:

Miss Lee's compliments to Mr Bates, for Wednesday evening, Nov. 18th, at 8 o'clock.

Addressed to a lady:

Miss Lee requests the pleasure of Miss Howard's company on Wednesday evening, Nov. 18th, at 8 o'clock.

For a ball, the above form, with the word *Dancing*, in the left hand corner.

Invitations to dinner or tea specify the entertainment thus:

Mrs Garret's compliments to Mr and Mrs Howard, and requests the pleasure of their company to dine (or take tea) on Wednesday, Nov. 6th, at 6 o'clock.

The form for answering, is –

Miss Howard accepts with pleasure Miss Lee's polite invitation for Wednesday evening.

or,

Miss Howard regrets that a prior engagement will prevent her accepting Miss Lee's polite invitation for Wednesday evening.

Mr and Mrs Howard's compliments to Mrs Garret, and accept with pleasure her kind invitation for Wednesday.

or,

Mrs Howard regrets that the severe illness of Mr Howard will render it impossible for either herself or Mr Howard to join Mrs Garret's party on Wednesday next.

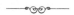

N O accomplishment within the scope of human knowledge is so beautiful in all its features as that of epistolary correspondence. Though distance, absence, and circumstances may separate the holiest alliances of friendship, or those who are bound together by the still stronger ties of affection, yet the power of interchanging thoughts, words, feelings, and sentiments, through the medium of letters, adds a sweetness to the pain of separation, renovating to life, and adding to happiness.

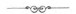

THE wide ocean may roll between those who have passed the social years of youth together, or the snow-capped Alps may rise in sublime grandeur, separating early associates; still young remembrances may be called up, and the paradise of memory made to bloom afresh with unwithered flowers of holy recollection.

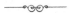

WITHOUT the ability to practise the refined art of epistolary correspondence, men would become cold and discordant: an isolated compound of misanthropy. They would fall off in forsaken fragments from the great bond of union which now adorns and beautifies all society. Absence, distance, and time would cut the silken cords of parental, brotherly, and even connubial affection. Early circumstances would be lost in forgetfulness, and the virtues of reciprocal friendship 'waste their sweetness on the desert air'.

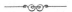

SINCE, then, the art and practice of letter-writing is productive of so much refined and social happiness, a laudable indulgence in it must ever be commendable. While it elevates the noble faculties of the mind, it also chastens the disposition, and improves those intellectual powers which would otherwise remain dormant and useless.

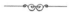

Notwithstanding the various beauties and pleasures attendant upon the accomplishment, yet there are many who have given it but a slight portion of their attention, and have, therefore, cause to blush at their own ignorance when necessity demands its practice. There is no better mode by which to test the acquirements of either a young lady or gentleman than from their letters.

Letters are among the most useful forms of composition. There are few persons, who can read or write at all, who do not frequently have occasion to write them; and an elegant letter is much more rare than an elegant specimen of any other kind of writing.

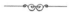

The more rational and elevated the topics are, on which you write, the less will you care for your letters being seen, or for paragraphs being read out of them; and where there is no need of any secrecy, it is best not to bind your friend by promises, but to leave it to her discretion.

CHAPTER XVI

Polite Deportment and Good Habits

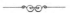

L ORD Chesterfield says, 'Good sense and good nature suggest civility in general; but in good breeding there are a thousand little delicacies which are established only by custom.' It is the knowledge and practice of such 'little delicacies' which constitutes the greatest charm of society.

M ANNER may be, and, in most cases, probably is, the cloak of the heart; this cloak may be used to cover defects, but is it not better so to conceal these defects, than to flaunt and parade them in the eyes of all whom we may meet?

M ANY persons plead a love of truth as an apology for rough manners, as if truth was never gentle and kind, but always harsh, morose, and forbidding. Surely good manners and a good conscience are no more inconsistent with each other than beauty and innocence, which are strikingly akin, and always look the better for companionship. Roughness and honesty are indeed sometimes found together in the same person, but he is a poor judge of human nature who takes ill-manners to be a guarantee of probity of character. Some persons object to politeness, that its language is unmeaning and false. But this is easily answered. A lie is not locked up in a phrase, but must exist, if at all, in the mind of the speaker. In the ordinary compliments of civilised life, there is no intention to deceive, and consequently no falsehood. Polite language is pleasant to the ear, and soothing to the heart, while rough words are just the reverse; and if not the product of ill temper, are very apt to produce it. The plainest of truths, let it be remembered, can be conveyed in civil speech, while the most malignant lies may find utterance, and often do, in the language of the fishmarket.

MANY ladies say, 'Oh, I am perfectly frank and outspoken; I never stop to mince words,' or, 'There is no affectation about me; all my actions are perfectly natural,' and, upon the ground of frankness, will insult and wound by rude language, and defend awkwardness and ill-breeding by the plea of 'natural manners'.

IF nature has not invested you with all the virtues which may be desirable in a lady, do not make your faults more conspicuous by thrusting them forward upon all occasions, and at all times. 'Assume a virtue if you have it not', and you will, in time, by imitation, acquire it.

B Y endeavouring to *appear* generous, disinterested, self-sacrificing, and amiable, the opposite passions will be brought
into subjection, first in the manner, afterwards in the heart. It
is not the desire to deceive, but the desire to please, which will
dictate such a course. When you hear one, who pretends to be
a lady, boast that she is rough, capricious, and gluttonous, you
may feel sure that she has never tried to conquer these faults,
or she would be ashamed, not proud, of them.

T HE way to make yourself pleasing to others, is to show
that you care for them. The whole world is like the miller
at Mansfield, 'who cared for nobody – no, not he – because
nobody cared for him'. And the whole world will serve you
so, if you give them the same cause. Let everyone, therefore,
see that you do care for them, by showing them, what Sterne
so happily calls, 'the small, sweet courtesies of life', those
courtesies in which there is no parade; whose voice is too still
to tease, and which manifest themselves by tender and affectionate looks, and little, kind acts of attention, giving others
the preference in every little enjoyment at the table, in the
field, walking, sitting, or standing.

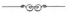

T HUS the first rule for a graceful manner is unselfish
consideration of others.

B Y endeavouring to acquire the habit of politeness, it
will soon become familiar, and sit on you with ease, if

not with elegance. Let it never be forgotten, that genuine politeness is a great fosterer of family love; it allays accidental irritation, by preventing harsh retorts and rude contradictions; it softens the boisterous, stimulates the indolent, suppresses selfishness, and by forming a habit of consideration for others, harmonises the whole. Politeness begets politeness, and brothers may be easily won by it, to leave off the rude ways they bring home from school or college. Sisters ought never to receive any little attention without thanking them for it, never to ask a favour of them but in courteous terms, never to reply to their questions in monosyllables, and they will soon be ashamed to do such things themselves. Both precept and example ought to be laid under contribution, to convince them that no one can have really good manners abroad, who is not habitually polite at home.

I f you wish to be a well-bred lady, you must carry your good manners everywhere with you. It is not a thing that can be laid aside and put on at pleasure. True politeness is uniform disinterestedness in trifles, accompanied by the calm self-possession which belongs to a noble simplicity of purpose; and this must be the effect of a Christian spirit running through all you do, or say, or think; and, unless you cultivate it and exercise it, upon all occasions and towards all persons, it will never be a part of yourself.

I t is not an art to be paraded upon public occasions, and neglected in everyday duties; nor should it, like a balldress, be carefully laid aside at home, trimmed, ornamented, and worn only when out. Let it come into every *thought*, and it will show forth in every *action*. Let it be the rule in the homeliest duties, and then it will set easily when in public, not in a stiff manner, like a garment seldom worn.

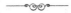

I WISH it were possible to convince every woman that politeness is a most excellent good quality; that it is a necessary ingredient in social comfort, and a capital assistant to actual prosperity. Like most good things, however, the word politeness is often misunderstood and misapplied; and before urging the practical use of that which it represents, it may be necessary to say what it means, and what it does not mean.

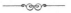

POLITENESS is not hypocrisy – cold-heartedness, or unkindness in disguise. There are persons who can smile upon a victim, and talk smoothly, while they injure, deceive, or betray. And they will take credit to themselves, that all has been done with the utmost *politeness*; that every tone, look, and action, has been in perfect keeping with the rules of good breeding. 'The words of their mouth are smoother than butter, but war is in their heart: their words are softer than oil, yet are they drawn swords.' Perish for ever and ever such spurious politeness as this!

POLITENESS is not servility. If it were so, a Russian serf would be a model of politeness. It is very possible for persons to be very cringing and obsequious, without a single atom of politeness; and it often happens that men of the most sturdy independence of character, are essentially polite in all their words, actions, and feelings. It were well for this to be fully understood, for many people will abstain from acts of real politeness, and even of common civility, for fear of damaging their fancied independence.

TRUE politeness, as I understand it, is kindness and courtesy of feeling brought into everyday exercise. It comprehends hearty goodwill towards everybody, thorough and constant good humour, an easy deportment, and obliging manners. Every person who cultivates such feelings, and takes no pains to conceal them, will necessarily be polite, though she may not exactly know it; while, on the other hand, a woman essentially morose and selfish, whatever may be her pretensions, must be very far from truly polite.

IT is very true there are those whose position in society compels them to observe certain rules of etiquette which pass for politeness. They bow or curtsey with a decent grace; shake hands with the precise degree of vigour which the circumstances of the case require; speak just at the right time, and in the required manner, and smile with elegant propriety. Not a tone, look, or gesture, is out of place; not a habit indulged which etiquette forbids; and yet, there will be wanting, after all, the secret charm of sincerity and heart kindness, which those outward signs are intended to represent; and, wanting which, we have only the form, without the essence, of politeness.

L ET me recommend, therefore, far beyond all the rules ever penned by teachers of etiquette, the cultivation of kind and loving feelings. Throw your whole soul into the lesson, and you will advance rapidly towards the perfection of politeness, for 'out of the abundance of the heart the mouth speaketh', and the movements of your form and the words you utter will follow faithfully the hidden springs of action within.

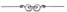

T HERE cannot be genuine good breeding to any happy degree, where there is not self-respect. It is that which imparts ease and confidence to our manners, and impels us, for our own sake, as well as for the sake of others, to behave becomingly as intelligent beings.

I T is a want of true politeness that introduces the discord and confusion which too often make our homes unhappy. A little consideration for the feelings of those whom we are bound to love and cherish, and a little sacrifice of our own wills, would, in multitudes of instances, make all the difference between alienation and growing affection. The principle of genuine politeness would accomplish this; and what a pity it is that those whose only spring of rational enjoyment is to be found at *home*, should miss that enjoyment by a disregard of little things, which, after all, make up the sum of human existence!

WHAT a large amount of actual discomfort in domestic life would be prevented, if all children were trained, both by precept and example, to the practice of common politeness! If they were taught to speak respectfully to parents, and brothers, and sisters, to friends, neighbours, and strangers, what bawlings, and snarlings would be stilled! If their behaviour within doors, and especially at the table, were regulated by a few of the common rules of good breeding, how much natural and proper disgust would be spared! If courtesy of demeanour, towards all whom they meet in field or highway, were instilled, how much more pleasant would be our town travels, and our rustic rambles! Every parent has a personal interest in this matter; and if every parent would but make the needful effort, a great degree of gross incivility, and consequent annoyance, would soon be swept away from our hearths and homes.

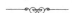

WHILST earnestly endeavouring to acquire true politeness, avoid that spurious imitation, affectation. It is to genuine politeness and good breeding, what the showy paste is to the pure diamond. It is the offspring of a sickly taste, a deceitful heart, and a sure proof of low breeding.

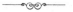

WITHOUT self-respect you will be apt to be both awkward and bashful; either of which faults are entirely incon-sistent with a graceful manner. Be careful that while you have sufficient self-respect to make your manner easy, it does not become arrogance and so engender insolence. Avoid sarcasm; it will, unconsciously to yourself, degenerate into pertness, and often downright rudeness. Do not be afraid to speak candidly, but temper candour with courtesy, and never let wit run into that satire that will wound deeply, whilst it amuses only slightly.

L ET your carriage be at once dignified and graceful. There are but few figures that will bear quick motion; with almost everyone its effect is that of a jerk, a most awkward movement. Let the feet, in walking or dancing, be turned out slightly; when you are seated, rest them both on the floor or a footstool. To sit with the knees or feet crossed or doubled up, is awkward and unladylike. Carry your arms, in walking, easily; never crossing them stiffly or swinging them beside you. When seated, if you are not sewing or knitting, keep your hands perfectly quiet. This, whilst one of the most difficult accomplishments to attain, is the surest mark of a lady. Do not fidget, playing with your rings, brooch, or any little article that may be near you; let your hands rest in an easy, natural position, perfectly quiet.

N EVER gesticulate when conversing; it looks theatrical, and is ill-bred; so are all contortions of the features, shrugging of shoulders, raising of the eyebrows, or hands.

W HEN you open a conversation, do so with a slight bow and smile, but be careful not to simper, and not to smile too often, if the conversation becomes serious.

NEVER point. It is excessively ill-bred.

AVOID exclamations; they are in excessively bad taste, and are apt to be vulgar words. A lady may express as much polite surprise or concern by a few simple, earnest words, or in her manner, as she can by exclaiming 'Good gracious!' 'Mercy!' or 'Dear me!'

REMEMBER that every part of your person and dress should be in perfect order before you leave the dressing room, and avoid all such tricks as smoothing your hair with your hand, arranging your curls, pulling the waist of your dress down, or settling your collar or sleeves.

AVOID lounging attitudes, they are indelicate, except in your own private apartment. Nothing but ill health will excuse them before company, and a lady had better keep her room if she is too feeble to sit up in the drawing room.

LET your deportment suit your age and figure; to see a tiny, fairy-like young girl, marching erect, stiff, and awkwardly, like a soldier on parade, is not more absurd than to see a middle-aged, portly woman, aping the romping, hoydenish manners of a schoolgirl.

L ET the movements be easy and flexible, and accord with the style of the lady.

L ET your demeanour be always marked by modesty and simplicity; as soon as you become forward or affected, you have lost your greatest charm of manner.

L ET your articulation be easy, clear, correct in accent, and suited in tone and emphasis to your discourse.

A VOID a muttering, mouthing, stuttering, droning, guttural, nasal, or lisping, pronunciation.

L ET your speech be neither too loud nor too low; but adjusted to the ear of your companion. Try to prevent the necessity of any person crying, 'What? What?'

A VOID a loquacious propensity; you should never occupy more than your share of the time, or more than is agreeable to others.

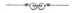

Beware of such vulgar interpolations as 'You know', 'You see', 'I'll tell you what'.

Pay a strict regard to the rules of grammar, even in private conversation. If you do not understand these rules, learn them, whatever be your age or station.

Though you should always speak pleasantly, do not mix your conversation with loud bursts of laughter.

Never indulge in uncommon words, or in Latin and French phrases, but choose the best understood terms to express your meaning.

Above all, let your conversation be intellectual, graceful, chaste, discreet, edifying, and profitable.

CHAPTER XVII

---❧❧❧---

Ballroom Etiquette

FOR THE HOSTESS

W HEN you have decided upon what evening you will give your ball, send out your invitations, a fortnight before the evening appointed. To ladies, word them –

Mrs L—

requests the pleasure of
Mrs G—'s company,
on Wednesday evening,
Jan 17th, at– 9 o'clock.

Dancing
The favour of an early
answer is requested

---❧❧❧---

To gentlemen –

Mrs L—'s *compliments to*
Mr R— for Wednesday evening,
Jan 17th, at– 9 o'clock.

Dancing
The favour of an early
answer is requested

If you are unmarried, put your mother's name with your own upon the cards. If you have a father or grown-up brother, let the invitations to the gentlemen go in his name.

In making your list for a ball, do not set down *all* of your 'dear five hundred friends'. The middle-aged (unless they come as chaperons), the serious, and the sober-minded, will not accept your invitation, and the two last named may consider it insulting to be invited to so frivolous an amusement. By the way, I do not agree with the straight-laced people, who condemn all such amusements. I agree with Madame Pilau. When the curé of her parish told her he was writing a series of sermons against dancing, she said to him: 'You are talking of what you do not understand. *You* have never been to a ball, *I* have; and I assure you there is no sin in the matter worthy of mention or notice.'

I F you really wish for dancing, you will accommodate your guests to your rooms, inviting one third more than they will hold, as about that number generally disappoint a ball-giver. If you wish to have a rush of people, and do not mind heat, crowding, and discomfort, to ensure an immense assembly (a ball to be talked about for its size only) then you may invite everybody who figures upon your visiting list.

O VER one hundred is a 'large ball', under that a 'ball', unless there are less than fifty guests, when it is merely a 'dance'.

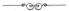

T HE directions given in chapter fifth for the arrangement of the dressing rooms will apply here, but your parlour, or ballroom, requires some attention. Have the carpets taken up two days before the evening of the ball, and the floor waxed. A smooth, polished floor is an absolute necessity for pleasant dancing. At one end of your ballroom, have a space partitioned off for the musicians. Leave, for their use, plenty of room, as silence or discord will come from a crowded orchestra. If your house is double, and you use the rooms on each side, place the musicians in the hall.

F OUR pieces of music is enough for a private ball, unless your rooms are very large. For one room a piano, violin, and violoncello makes a good band.

Y OU must have your rooms well ventilated if you wish to avoid fainting and discomfort.

T O secure a really brilliant ball, pay considerable attention to the arrangement of your ballroom. In Paris this arrangement consists in turning the room, for the evening, into a perfect garden. Every corner is filled with flowers. Wreaths, bouquets, baskets, and flowering plants in moss-covered pots. With brilliant light, and taste in the details of arranging them, this profusion of flowers produces an exquisitely beautiful effect, and harmonises perfectly with the light dresses, cheerful faces, and gay music. The pleasure of your guests, as well as the beauty of the rooms, will be increased by the elegance of your arrangements; their beauty will be heightened by brilliant light, and by judicious management a scene of fairy-like illusion may be produced.

N OT only in the ballroom itself, but in the hall, supper-room, and dressing rooms, place flowers. A fine effect is produced, by placing a screen, covered with green and flowers, before the space set apart for the musicians. To hear the music proceeding from behind this floral embankment, and yet have the scraping and puffing men invisible, adds very much to the illusion of the scene.

I N the dressing rooms have, at least, two servants for each. Let them take the cloaks and hoods, and put a numbered ticket upon each bundle, handing the duplicate number to the lady or gentleman owning it.

I T is best to have the supper-room upon the same floor as the ballroom. The light dresses, worn upon such occasions, suffer severely in passing up and down a crowded staircase.

H AVE a number of double cards written or printed with a list of the dances, arranged in order, upon one side, and a space for engagements upon the other. Attach a small pencil to each. Let a waiter stand at the entrance to the ballroom, and hand a card to each guest as they pass in.

T HE first strain of music must be a march; then follows a quadrille, then a waltz. Other dances follow in any order you prefer until the fourteenth, which should be the march which announces supper. If you throw open the supper-room, early, and the guests go out when they wish, the march may be omitted. Twenty-one to twenty-four dances are sufficient. Have an interval of ten minutes after each one.

T HE supper-room should be thrown open at midnight, and remain open until your last guest has departed.

Let it be brilliantly lighted, and have plenty of waiters in attendance.

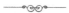

THERE can be no rule laid down for the supper. It may be hot or heavily iced. It may consist entirely of confectionery, or it may include the bill of fare for a hotel table. One rule you must observe; have abundance of everything. Other entertainments may be given upon economical principles, but a ball cannot. Light, attendance, supper, every detail must be carefully attended to, and a ball must be an expensive luxury.

AT a ball-supper everyone stands up. The waiters will hand refreshment from the tables to the gentlemen, who, in turn, wait upon the ladies.

YOU must bring forth your whole array of smiles, when you perform the part of hostess in a ballroom. As your guests will come dropping in at all hours, you must hover near the door to greet each one entering. There will be many strangers amongst the gentlemen. Miss G. will bring her fiancé. Miss L., her brother, just returned, after ten years' absence, from India. Miss R. introduces her cousin, in the city for a week. Miss M., as a belle, will, perhaps, take the liberty of telling some ten or twelve of her most devoted admirers where she may be seen on the evening of your ball, and, though strangers, they will, one after another, bow over your hand. To each and every one you must extend the amiable greeting due to an invited guest. If you are the only lady of the house, your duties will, indeed, be laborious. You must be everywhere at the same moment. Not a guest must pass unwelcomed. You must introduce partners to all the wall-flowers. You must see that every set is made up before the music commences. Each guest must be introduced to a proper partner for every dance, and not one frown, one pettish word, one look of fatigue, one sigh of utter weariness must disturb your smiling serenity. You must be ready to chat cheerfully with every bore who detains you, when crossing the room, to make up a set of quadrilles in a minute's time; listen patiently to the sighing lover, whose fair one is engaged fifty times during twenty dances; secure a good dancer for each longing belle; do the same for the beaux; yet you must never be hurried, worried, or fatigued.

I F there are several ladies, a mother and two or three daughters, for instance, divide the duties. Let one receive the guests, another arrange the sets, a third introduce couples, and a fourth pair off the talkers. A brother or father will be a treasure in a ballroom, as the standing of sets can be better managed by a gentleman than a lady.

N ONE of the ladies who give the ball should dance until every fair guest has a partner.

O NE of your duties will be to see that no young ladies lose their supper for want of an escort to ask them to go out. You may give the hint to an intimate gentleman friend, if there is no brother or father to take the duty, introduce him to the disconsolate damsel, and send her off happy. If all the guests go to the supper-room when it is first thrown open, you must be the last to leave the ballroom. For the hostess to take the lead to the supper-room, leaving her guests to pair off, and follow as they please, is in very bad taste.

I F you announce supper by a march, many of your guests will remain in the ballroom, to promenade, avoid the crowd at the first table, and indulge in a tête-à-tête conversation. These will afterwards go out, in pairs, when the first crush in the refreshment-room is over.

I F, by accident or negligence, you miss an introduction to any of your gentlemen guests, you may still speak to them if you wish. It is your privilege as hostess to introduce yourself, and invite any gentleman to dance with you, or offer to introduce him to a partner. In the latter case he ought to mention his name, but if he omits to do so, you may ask it.

T HERE has been a custom introduced in some of our large cities lately, which is an admirable one for a private ball. It is to hire, for the evening, a public hall. This includes the dressing room, supper-room, every comfort, and saves you from the thousand annoyances which are certain to follow a ball in a private house. You hire the hall and other rooms, the price including light, hire a band of music, and order a supper at a confectioner's, hiring from his establishment all the china, glass, and silver you will want. In this case you must enclose in every invitation a ticket to admit your friend's party, to prevent loungers from the street coming in, uninvited.

Y OU will, perhaps, find the actual outlay of money greater, when you thus hire your ballroom, but you will save more than the difference in labour, annoyance, and the injury to your house. You secure a better room than any parlour, you have the floor waxed and polished without the trouble of taking up your carpets. You save all the dreadful labour of cleaning up the house the next day, as well as that of preparation.

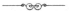

Y OU can, if you wish, invite a few friends to a late dinner with you, and all proceed to the ballroom together. You must be the first to enter the room, the last to leave it, and every duty is the same as if you were at home; the ballroom is, in fact, your own house, for the evening.

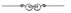

I F you wish your guests to come in costume for a fancy ball, name the character of the entertainment in your invitation.

CHAPTER XVIII

Ballroom Etiquette

FOR THE GUEST

A s in every other case where hospitality is extended to you by invitation, you must send your answer as soon as possible, accepting or declining the civility.

I N preparing a costume for a ball, choose something very light. Heavy, dark silks are out of place in a ballroom, and black should be worn in no material but lace. For a married lady, rich silk of some light colour, trimmed with flowers, lace, or tulle; white silk plain, or lace over satin, make an exquisite toilette. Jewels are perfectly appropriate; also feathers in the *coiffure*.

F OR the young lady, pure white or light colours should be worn, and the most appropriate dress is of some thin material made over silk, white, or the same colour as the outer dress. Satin or velvet are entirely out of place on a young lady. Let the *coiffure* be of flowers or ribbons, never feathers, and but very little jewellery is becoming to an unmarried lady. All ladies must wear boots or slippers of satin, white, black, or the colour of the dress. White are the most appropriate; black, the most becoming to the foot. White kid gloves, full trimmed, a fine lace trimmed handkerchief, and a fan, are indispensable. Be very careful, when dressing for a ball, that the hair is firmly fastened, and the *coiffure* properly adjusted. Nothing is more annoying than to have the hair loosen or the headdress fall off in a crowded ballroom.

Y OUR first duty, upon entering the room, is to speak to your hostess. After a few words of greeting, turn to the other guests.

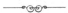

A T a private ball, no lady will refuse an introduction to a gentleman. It is an insult to her hostess, implying that her guests are *not gentlemen*. It is optional with the lady whether to continue or drop the acquaintance after the ball is over, but for that evening, however disagreeable, etiquette requires her to accept him for *one* dance, if she is disengaged, and her hostess requests it. At a public ball, it is safest to decline all introductions made by the master of ceremonies, though, as before, such acquaintances are not binding after the evening is over.

B E very careful how you refuse to dance with a gentleman. A prior engagement will, of course, excuse you, but if you plead fatigue, or really feel it, do not dance the set with another gentleman; it is most insulting, though sometimes done. On the other hand, be careful that you do not engage yourself twice for the same quadrille. In a polka or valse, you may do this, saying, 'I will dance the second half with you, but have a prior engagement for the first.' Then, after a few rounds with your first partner, say to him that you are engaged for the remainder of the dance, resume your seat, and your second partner will seek you.

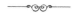

L ET your manner in a ballroom be quiet. It looks very badly to see a lady endeavouring to attract attention by her boisterous manner, loud talking, or over-active dancing. Do not drag through dances as if you found them wearisome; it is an insult to your partner, but while you are cheerful and animated, be ladylike and dignified in your deportment.

A T the end of each dance, your partner will offer his arm, and conduct you to a seat; then bow, and release him from further attendance, as he may be engaged for the next dance.

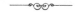

W HEN invited to dance, hand your ball card to the gentleman, who will put his name in one of the vacant places.

I F you wish to go to the supper-room, accept the invitation that will be made, after the dances whilst it is open, but do not remain there long. You may be keeping your escort from other engagements.

I F you are accompanied by a gentleman, besides your father or brother, remember he has the right to the first dance, and also will expect to take you in to supper. Do not let anyone else interfere with his privilege.

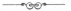

I F you wish, during the evening, to go to the dressing room to arrange any part of your dress, request the gentleman with whom you are dancing to escort you there. He will wait for you at the door, and take you back to the ballroom. Do not detain him any longer than is necessary. Never leave the ballroom, for any such purpose, alone, as there are always gentlemen near and round the door, and it looks very badly to see a lady, unattended, going through a crowd of gentlemen.

I T is best at a ball, to dance only every other dance, as over-fatigue, and probably a flushed face, will follow too much dancing. Decline the intermediate ones, on the plea of fatigue, or fear of fatigue.

NEVER go into the supper-room with the same gentleman twice. You may go more than once, if you wish for an ice or glass of water (surely no lady wants two or three *suppers*) but do not tax the same gentleman more than once, even if he invites you after each dance.

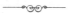

NO lady of taste will carry on a flirtation in a ballroom, so as to attract remark. Be careful, unless you wish your name coupled with his, how you dance too often with the same gentleman.

IF you are so unfortunate as, forgetting a prior engagement, to engage yourself to two gentlemen for the same dance, decline dancing it altogether, or you will surely offend one of them.

NEVER press forward to take the lead in a quadrille, and if others, not understanding the figures, make confusion, try to get through without remark. It is useless to attempt to teach them, as the music, and other sets, will finish the figure long before you can teach and dance it. Keep your temper, refrain from all remark, and endeavour to make your partner forget, in your cheerful conversation, the annoyances of the dance.

THERE is much that is exhilarating in the atmosphere of a ballroom. The light, music, company, and even dancing itself, are all conducive to high spirits; be careful that this flow of spirits does not lead you into hoydenism and rudeness. Guard your actions and your tongue, that you may leave the room as quietly and gracefully as you enter it.

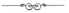

AVOID confidential conversation in a ballroom. It is out of season, and in excessively bad taste.

BE modest and reserved, but avoid bashfulness. It looks like a schoolgirl, and is invariably awkward.

NEVER allow your partner, though he may be your most intimate friend, to converse in a low tone, or in any way assume a confidential or lover-like air at a ball. It is in excessively bad taste, and gives annoyance frequently, as others suppose such low-toned remarks may refer to them.

DANCE as others do. It has a very absurd look to take every step with dancing-school accuracy, and your partner will be the first one to notice it. A quadrille takes no more steps than a graceful walk.

NEVER stand up to dance in a quadrille, unless you are perfectly familiar with the figures, depending upon your partner to lead you through. You will probably cause utter confusion in the set, annoy the others forming it, and make yourself appear absurd.

----◦✑◉✒◦----

NO young lady should go to a ball, without the protection of a married lady, or an elderly gentleman.

----◦✑◉✒◦----

NEVER cross a ballroom alone.

----◦✑◉✒◦----

NEVER remain in a ballroom until all the company have left it, or even until the last set. It is ill-bred, and looks as if you were unaccustomed to such pleasures, and so desirous to prolong each one. Leave while there are still two or three sets to be danced. Do not accept any invitation for these late dances, as the gentleman who invites you may find out your absence too late to take another partner, and you will thus deprive him of the pleasure of dancing.

CHAPTER XIX

Places of Amusement

Do not accept an invitation to visit any place of public amusement, with a gentleman with whom you are but slightly acquainted, unless there is another lady also invited. You may, as a young lady, go with a relative or your fiancé, without a chaperon, but not otherwise.

Having received an invitation which it is proper for you to accept, write an answer immediately, appointing an hour for your escort to call for you, and be sure that you are ready in good season. To arrive late is not only annoying to those near your seat, whom you disturb when you enter, but it is ill-bred; you will be supposed to be someone who is unable to come early, instead of appearing as a lady who is mistress of her own time.

The Theatre – Here you must wear your bonnet, though you may throw aside your cloak or shawl, if you desire it. Your escort will pass to your seats first, and then turn and offer his hand to lead you to your own. Once seated, give your attention entirely to the actors whilst the curtain is up – to your companion when it is down.

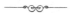

Do not look round the house with your glass. A lady's deportment should be very modest in a theatre. Avoid carefully every motion, or gesture that will attract attention. To flirt a fan, converse in whispers, indulge in extravagant gestures of merriment or admiration, laugh loudly or clap your hands together, are all excessively vulgar and unladylike. Never turn your head to look at those seated behind you, or near you.

If you speak to your companion while the curtain is up, lower your voice, that you may not disturb others interested in the conversation on the stage.

The Opera – Here you should wear full dress, an opera cloak, and either a headdress, or dressy bonnet of some thin material. Your gloves must be of kid, white, or some very light tint to suit your dress. Many dress for the opera as they would for the theatre; but the beauty of the house is much enhanced by each lady contributing her full dress toilette to the general effect.

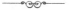

If you go to the dressing room, leave your hood and shawl in the care of the woman in waiting, whom you must fee when she returns them to you.

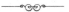

AVOID handling the play bills, as the printing ink will soil your gloves in a few minutes, making your hands appear very badly for the rest of the evening.

YOU should be in your seat at the opera before the overture commences.

NEVER converse during the performance. Even the lowest toned remark will disturb a real lover of music, and these will be near you on all sides. Exclamations of admiration, 'Exquisite!' 'Beautiful!' or 'Lovely!' are in the worst taste. Show your appreciation by quiet attention to every note, and avoid every exclamation or gesture.

IN our new opera houses there are rooms for promenade, and between the acts your escort may invite you to walk there. You may accept the invitation with perfect propriety. He will leave the box first and then offer his hand to you. In the lobby take his arm, and keep it until you return to the box. If you have taken your cloak or shawl to your seat, leave them there during your promenade. Return to your seat when the gong sounds the recall, that you may not disturb others after the next act commences.

I N walking up and down in the promenading saloon, you may pass and repass friends. Bow the first time you meet them, but not again.

I F you meet your gentlemen friends there, bow, but do not stop to speak. They may join you for once round the room, then allow them to leave you. Your escort will feel justly offended if you allow any other gentlemen to engross your attention entirely when he has invited you to the entertainment.

C ONCERTS – Here, as at the opera, you may wear a bonnet or not, as you will. Go early to the hall, unless you have secured a seat, and then, be in time for the first song. If you are unavoidably late, enter quietly, and take a seat near the door. It is very rude to push forward to the front of the hall, and either crowd those upon the benches, or force some gentleman to offer you his place. If the hall is so crowded that even the back seats are full, and a gentleman offers you his place, you should thank him before accepting it.

A GAIN, I repeat, do not converse, or disturb those around you by exclamations or gesticulations.

L ECTURES – Two ladies may attend a lecture, unaccompanied by a gentleman, without attracting attention.

THE dress, bonnet, and cloak, worn in the street, should be worn in a lecture-room, as these are, by no means, occasions for full dress.

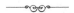

IF you return at an early hour from any place of amusement, invite your escort into the house upon your arrival there, and lay aside your bonnet and shawl. If you keep them on, he will conclude that you expect him to shorten his visit. If it is late when you reach home, he will probably decline your invitation to enter. If, however, he accepts it, do not lay aside your shawl, and he will soon leave you.

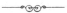

IF he asks permission to call in the morning, you must, unless prevented by an imperative engagement, remain at home to see him.

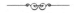

IF at the theatre, opera, or in a concert-room, you see an acquaintance, you are not expected to recognise her, unless near enough to speak. A lady must not bow to anyone, even her own sister, across a theatre or concert-room.

CHAPTER XX

Accomplishments

I N the present age, when education is within the reach of all, both rich and poor, every lady will endeavour to become, not only well educated, but accomplished. It is not, as some will assert, a waste of time or money. Not only the fingers, voice, and figure are improved, but the heart and intellect will become refined, and the happiness greatly increased.

T AKE the young lady after a solid basis has been laid in her mind of the more important branches of education, and rear upon that basis the structure of lighter education – the accomplishments. To cultivate these, disregarding the more solid information, is to build your castle without any foundation, and make it, not only absurd, but unsteady. The pleasure of hearing from a lady a *cavatina* executed in the most finished manner, will be entirely destroyed, if her first spoken words after the performance are vulgar, or her sentence ungrammatical.

A LADY without her piano, or her pencil, her library of French, German, or Italian authors, her fancy work and tasteful embroideries, is now rarely met with, and it is right that such arts should be universal. No woman is fitted for society until she dances well; for home, unless she is perfect mistress of needlework; for her own enjoyment, unless she has at least one accomplishment to occupy thoughts and fingers in her hours of leisure.

FIRST upon the list of accomplishments, comes the art of conversing well. It is always ready. Circumstances in society will constantly throw you into positions where you can use no other accomplishment. You will not have a musical instrument within reach, singing would be out of place, your fancy work at home, on many occasions, and then you can exert your most fascinating as well as useful accomplishment, the art of conversing well.

LITTLE culture, unfortunately, is bestowed upon this accomplishment, which, beyond all others, promotes the happiness of home, enlivens society, and improves the minds of both speaker and listener. How many excellent women are deficient in the power of expressing themselves well, or, indeed, of expressing themselves at all! How many minds 'cream and mantle' from the want of energy to pour themselves out in words! On the other hand, how some, equally well intentioned, drown the very senses in their torrent of remarks, which dashes, like a waterfall, into a sombre pool of *ennui* below!

O NE lady will enter society, well dressed, well looking, polite; she does not intend to chill it by her presence; yet her absence is found a relief. She takes her place as if she considered it sufficient to dress and look well. She brings no stock to the community of ideas. Her eyes return no response to the discourse which is going on. When you have once glanced at her, she becomes a mere expletive in the company.

A NOTHER one will be found a talker. She is like a canary bird; when others begin to speak, she hurries in her remarks, in an accompaniment. Her voice must be uppermost; conversation becomes a contest who can speak the most rapidly. The timid and modest retire from the encounter – she has the field to herself. She goes on, without mercy; the voice of a siren would fatigue, if heard continually. Others revolt at the injustice of the monopoly, and the words fall on ears that would be deaf if they could.

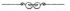

T HESE are extreme cases; there are many other minor errors. The higher qualities of conversation must undoubtedly be based upon the higher qualities of the mind; then it is, indeed, a privilege to commune with others.

T O acquire the power of thus imparting the highest pleasure by conversational powers, attention must be paid to literature. I am supposing the solid foundation of a good education already laid, but by literature, I do not mean only that class of it which is taught at school.

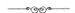

R EADING, at the present day, is too much confined to light literature. I would not speak against this. The modern novels, and the poets of all ages, are good reading, but let them be taken in moderation, and varied by something more solid. Let them be the *dessert* to the more substantial *dinner* of history, travels, and works of a like nature.

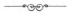

I NDEPENDENT of the strength and polish given to the mind by a thorough course of reading, there is another reason why a lady should devote some portion of her time to it; she cannot do without it. She may, lacking this, pass through life respectably, even elegantly; but she cannot take her part in a communing with superior minds; she may enjoy, in wondering, the radiance of their intelligence; but the wondering must be composed, in part, of amazement at her own folly, in not having herself sought out the treasure concealed in the fathomless depths of books. She cannot truly enjoy society, with this art neglected. She may, for a few brief years, be the ornament of the drawing room; but it must be, like many other ornaments there, in still life; she can never be the companion of the intellectual; and the time is gone by, when women, with all their energies excited, will be contented to be the mere plaything of brother, husband, or father. Still it is not to the erudite, nor to the imaginative only, that it is given to please in conversation.

It is, in general, a wise rule, and one which will tend much to ensure your comfort through life, to avoid disclosures to others of family affairs. I do not mean to recommend reserve, or art; to friends and relations, too great frankness can hardly be practised; but, with acquaintance, the less our own circumstances are discussed, the happier, and the more dignified will our commerce with them continue. On the same principle, let the concerns of others be touched upon with delicacy, or, if possible, passed over in silence; more especially those details which relate to strictly personal or family affairs. Public deeds are, of course, public property. But personal affairs are private; and there is a want of true good breeding, a want of consideration and deference, in speaking freely of them, even if your friend is unconscious of the liberty taken.

It seems paradoxical to observe that the art of listening well forms a part of the duty of conversation. To give up the whole of your attention to the person who addresses himself to you, is sometimes a heavy tax, but it is one which we must pay for the privileges of social life, and an early practice will render it an almost involuntary act of good breeding; whilst consideration for others will give this little sacrifice a merit and a charm.

To listen well is to make an unconscious advance in the power of conversing. In listening we perceive in what the interest, in what the failure of others consists; we become, too, aware of our own deficiencies, without having them taught through the medium of humiliation. We find ourselves often more ignorant than we could have supposed possible. We learn, by a very moderate attention to the sort of topics which please, to form a style of our own. The 'art of conversation' is an unpleasant phrase. The power of conversing well is least agreeable when it assumes the character of an *art*.

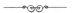

I N listening, a well-bred lady will gently sympathise with the speaker; or, if needs must be, differ, as gently. Much character is shown in the act of listening. Some people appear to be in a violent hurry whilst another speaks; they hasten on the person who addresses them, as one would urge on a horse – with incessant 'Yes, yes, very good – indeed – proceed!' Others sit, on the full stare, eyes fixed as those of an owl, upon the speaker. Others will receive every observation with a little hysterical giggle. But all these vices of manner may be avoided by a gentle attention and a certain calm dignity of manner, based upon a reflective, cultivated mind.

O BSERVATION, reading, and study, will form the groundwork for good powers of conversation, and the more you read, study, and see, the more varied and interesting will be your topics.

A YOUNG lady should consider music as one branch of her education, inferior, in importance, to most of those studies which are pointed out to her, but attainable in a sufficient degree by the aid of time, perseverance, and a moderate degree of instruction. Begun early, and pursued steadily, there is ample leisure in youth for the attainment of a science, which confers more cheerfulness, and brings more pleasure than can readily be conceived.

A YOUNG lady should be able to play with taste, correctness, and readiness, upon the general principle that a well-educated woman should do all things well. This, I should suppose, is in the power of most persons; and it may be attained without loss of health, of time, or any sacrifice of an important nature. She should consider it as an advantage, a power to be employed for the gratification of others, and to be indulged with moderation and good sense for her own resource, as a change of occupation.

M USIC has an influence peculiar to itself. It can allay the irritation of the mind; it cements families, and makes a home, which might sometimes be monotonous, a scene of pleasant excitement. Pursued as a recreation, it is gentle, rational, ladylike. Followed as a sole object, it loses its charm, because we perceive it is then over-rated. The young lady who comes modestly forward, when called upon as a performer, would cease to please, were she, for an instant, to assume the air and confidence of a professional musician. There is a certain style and manner – confined now to second-rate performers, for the highest and most esteemed dispense with it – there is an effort and a dash, which disgust in the lady who has bad taste enough to assume them.

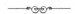

A ND, whilst I am on this topic, let me remark that there is a great deal in the *choice* of music, in the selection of its character, its suitability to your feelings, style, and taste, and this especially with respect to vocal music.

M USIC is the greatest, best substitute for conversation. It has many merits, in this light. It can never provoke angry retort; it can never make enemies; it can injure no one's character by slander; and in playing and singing one can commit no indiscretion.

M USIC is a most excellent amusement, and, in society, an indispensable one. It aids conversation by occasionally interrupting it for a short period, to be renewed with a new impetus. It makes the most delightful recreation for the home circle, varying the toil and trouble of the father's or husband's working day, by the pleasures of the evening made by music's power to glide smoothly and swiftly.

T HERE are but few persons who are entirely without a love for music, even if they do not understand it. They will be borne along upon the waves of a sweet melody to high, pure thoughts, often to delicious memories.

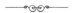

THE piano is, at the present day, the most popular instrument in society. The harp has ceased to be fashionable, though it is sometimes heard. The latter is a most beautiful accompaniment for the voice, but requires a large room, as, in a small one, it will sound stringy and harsh.

THE guitar, while it makes a very pleasant accompaniment for the voice, has also the advantage of being easily carried from place to place.

IT requires as much judgement to select proper instrumental pieces for a parlour performance, as you would display in a choice of songs. Page after page of black, closely printed notes, will drive those who see them from the piano. They may be executed in the most finished style, but they are not suited to general society. In their place, for practice, or for a musical soirée, where everyone puts forth her best musical powers, they are appropriate, and will give pleasure, but they are not suited for a mixed party. When asked to play, choose, if you will, a brilliant, showy piece, but let it be short. It is better still to make no attempt at display, but simply try to please, selecting the music your own judgement tells you is best suited to your audience.

A VOID the loud, thumping style, and also the over-solemn style.

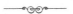

B E sure, before you accept any invitation to play, that you know perfectly the piece you undertake. It is better to play the simplest airs in a finished, faultless manner, than to play imperfectly the most brilliant variations.

A VOID movement at the piano. Swinging the body to and fro, moving the head, rolling the eyes, raising the hands too much, are all bad tricks, and should be carefully abstained from.

W ITH respect to drawing, modelling, or any pursuits of the same nature, so much depends on taste and oppor-tunity, and they are so little the accomplishments of society that they require but few of those restrictions which music, in its use and abuse, demands. Drawing, like music, should be cultivated early. Its advantages are the habits of perse-verance and occupation, which it induces; and the additional delight which it gives to the works, both of nature and of art. Like music, it gives independence – independence of society. The true lover of the arts has a superiority over the indif-ferent, and, if she be not better prepared for society, is much better fitted for retirement than those who are not so happily endowed with tastes, when in moderation, so innocent and beneficial.

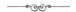

THERE is no accomplishment more graceful, pleasing, healthy, and ladylike, than that of riding well. Avoiding, at the same time, timidity and the 'fast' style, keeping within the bounds of elegant propriety, gracefully yielding to the guidance of your escort, and keeping your seat easily, yet steadily, are all points to be acquired.

To ride well is undoubtedly an admirable qualification for a lady, as she may be as feminine in the saddle as in the ballroom or home circle. It is a mistaken idea to suppose that to become an accomplished horse-woman a lady must unsex herself. But she must have a reserve in her manner, that will prevent contamination from the intercourse which too much riding may lead to. To hunt, or follow the field sports, in a pursuit which is the track of blood, disgusts the true admirer of gentle breeding. And such diversions will certainly result in a coarseness of manner and expression, growing upon the fair equestrian slowly but surely. A harsh voice, loud tone, expressions suited only to manly lips, but unconsciously copied, will follow her devotion to the unfeminine pursuit.

NOTHING is more revolting than a woman who catches the tone and expressions of men. To hear the slang of jockeyism from female lips, is very offensive, yet ladies who mix in field sports are liable, nay, almost certain, to fall into a style of conversation which is ten times worse than the coarsest terms from the lips of a man. Instances there are, of the fairest of our sex, from a fondness for such diversions, and a habitual participation in such society, becoming hard, bold, and disgusting, even whilst retaining all their female loveliness of person.

A LADY, unless she lives in the most retired parts of the country, should never ride alone, and even then she will be awkwardly placed, in case of accident, without an escort. In the cities, not only is it unfeminine, but positively dangerous, for a lady to ride unaccompanied by a gentleman, or a manservant.

A T the period for which these hints are intended, the Modern Languages should form a portion of acquirement. As in music, an intelligent and assiduous girl may, I believe, acquire an adequate degree of proficiency in French, German, and Italian, without having been abroad, though a foreign tour will be of the greatest use in the acquisition of the accent and niceties of each tongue. With respect to French, it is no doubt essential to comfort to understand it; it is one of the attributes of a lady to speak it well; still, it is not indispensable to speak it so well that the American lady is mistaken for a Parisian. This, which but seldom happens, can only be acquired, in most cases, by a residence abroad. But French is thoroughly and grammatically taught in America. It is only the habit of speaking, the idioms and niceties, which cannot be acquired except by converse with a native.

THERE are hundreds of competent instructors in this country, French ladies and gentlemen amongst the number, who form classes for conversation and familiarising their pupils with these very idioms. After availing herself of such advantages, a young lady will find that a very short residence abroad will improve and facilitate her French conversation.

MUCH, however, will depend upon how you use the opportunities within your reach. There are many opportunities of practice in large towns; and foreigners give all facilities, by their readiness to converse, their good nature in listening, and in helping the beginner by kind hints. If a young lady, with simplicity, good breeding, and good taste, endeavours to speak whenever she has an opportunity, words will come as if by intuition. Do not think of by-standers and lookers-on; think only of the individual to whom you are addressing yourself. If possible, be not abashed by one or two errors at the first plunge – swim on till you have confidence. The effort, I grant, is great, and it may be obviated by a foreign education; but where this is impossible, the freedom acquired will more than repay the exertion.

IN foreign literature, walk carefully, and if you have an older, wiser head than your own to point out the best paths, improve the advantage.

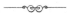

Oneꜱᴇ cannot help deeming it a great era in education that German is cultivated as well as Italian and French, and that stores of literature are opened, to vary the delights of intellect, and to give freshness and interest to the studies of youth. The rapture with which the works of Schiller are perused in the original, seems to repay the hours devoted to German; and I am sure the perusal of Tasso, or of the Aristodemo of Monti, would reward the study of Italian, were not the acquisition of that exquisite language of itself a source of poetic pleasure.

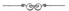

Aʟᴀᴅʏ in society must, if she would not grow utterly weary in company, know how to dance. It has been the practice among many excellent people to represent the ballroom as a 'pitfall covered with flowers'; a sheet of breaking ice; above, all gaiety and motion; below, all darkness and danger. It may be that to some minds the ballroom may be replete with temptations; but there are minds which find temptations everywhere. The innocent may be innocent, nay, the pious may feel devout, even in a ballroom. There is nothing immoral or wrong in dancing; it is the tendency of youth to dance – it is the first effort of a child – the first natural recreation. It seems so natural that I confess I am always doubtful of the sincerity of those young ladies who profess to dislike the ballroom.

Iɴ the present day, you must understand how to move gracefully through quadrilles, to dance polka, Schottische,

Varsovienne, and waltz. To these you may add great variety of dances, each season, probably, bringing a new one.

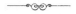

Dancing is an exercise which has been practised by mankind from the most remote ages. With the Egyptians, Assyrians, and Persians, the founders of the three great empires of the ancient world, dancing was the favourite exercise or accomplishment, and the practice was not less prevalent among their successors in power and importance, the Greeks and Romans. The Jews, also, we learn from Scripture, were strongly attached to the exercise at all periods of their history.

At the present day, almost every people that exist, whether barbarous or civilised, has its own form of dancing. It is this universality of the exercise that makes dancing a subject of importance. Being so extensively practised, it must be the instrument either of good or evil to the human race.

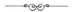

It is one of the most healthful and elegant amusements, and cannot be too highly recommended. Among a rude and dissolute people it may degenerate into something worthy of condemnation; but all the blessings we have are similarly liable to abuse, and it would be most unjust to condemn a cheerful domestic amusement, merely because it has, at times, been degraded by people of low, vulgar, immoral tastes. By all physicians, dancing, when pursued in moderation, is recommended as highly conducive to bodily health; and it may be truly said, that, allied with music, nothing is more conducive to *mental* health, more calculated to drive away melancholy, and put the whole temper into good humour.

D ANCING is the poetry of motion. It must be performed with ease and grace, and always with a perfect regard for propriety of movement.

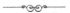

O NE of the most delightful accomplishments which a lady can possess, and one which is unfortunately but little cultivated, is the art of reading aloud well; reading with expression, taste, animation, and correctness; and this art once acquired, let her also be able to recite well.

L ONG lectures may be given upon elocution, but the advice can be condensed into two directions. First, be sure you pronounce, accent, and enunciate every word correctly; then, throw your whole soul into the words. Study your author carefully, that you may know precisely what he means by each expression, and then try to bury your personal identity, to become, for the time, the character you represent.

O NE of the most delightful ways to spend a social evening, is to devote it to dramatic literature. Invite only guests who read well, or who are really interested listeners, and select a play, or scenes from several plays, and cast the parts among your guests. All jealousy must be put aside, and tonight's Hamlet must condescend to direct Richard to 'Stand by, my lord, and let the coffin pass,' tomorrow.

A FTER a few meetings, the peculiar talent of each reader will be recognised, and you can select your tragedy hero, comedy hero, queen, chambermaid, and other members of the force, with a view to the display of each one's best powers. Vary the entertainment by reciting monologues and dialogues. A whole play will often be found tiresome; it is best to select several scenes, keeping up the thread of the plot, and introducing the best characters, and leave out what is mere interlude, and dispense with some of the subordinate characters.

L EAVE one end of the room entirely vacant for the readers. You will find it more interesting to have the readers stand, and use some little motion; the words will flow more easily, the expressions come more forcibly if the appropriate gesture is made. Love scenes will, of course, require delicate handling, and embracing can be easily omitted; neither would I recommend the action of a duelling scene, or a murder, but merely to add gesture enough to give interest to both readers and audience.

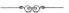

Y OU will find some little difficulty from bashfulness, and the 'don't like to' people at first, but soon you will discover with delight how many of your friends possess the talent for reading well, and never knew it themselves.

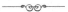

Y OU will do well to take a few lessons in elocution, but you need not fear to read if you have never made the accomplishment a study. With a correct knowledge of your own language, and a love for fine writing, you will soon read well.

G IVE to every part you undertake, the full effect intended by the writer. Do not throw all your energy, your whole soul, into a leading part at one time, and slight a subordinate character at another. If you have but five words to read, read them as they would be spoken were you the character you represent for the time. To hear a splendidly written, tragic burst of passion read in a weak, whining voice, is no worse than to have a few simple words from a servant's lips delivered with the gesture and emphasis suited to a Medea or Lady Macbeth.

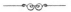

I SHALL be condemned by many serious and well-judging persons, if I say one word in favour of private theatricals; yet, as it appears to me, there are in these diversions some advantages which are not to be found to excuse the waltz, or the polka, or the ballet, or the hunting field. In private theatricals there is the possibility of *some* benefit. The study of the finest dramatists, especially of Shakespeare, is not likely to demoralise the mind, or to cool the enthusiasm for what is good. We can scarcely know too well those works which have tended more to form character than any collection of any kind whatsoever.

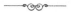

PRIVATE theatricals should, however, be regulated with much judgement. I see no reason to restrict too severely talent of this kind where it exists, any more than to crush a dawning taste for the other fine arts. What we have to do is to raise and direct it; never to let it occupy too much time, nor to become the business of life; never to let it infringe upon duties; never to allow it to lead us into an unreasonable, and, therefore, criminal expense. Our ancestors were content to strew their stage at the end of their halls with rushes, and to hang up the name of the scene, instead of a scene, before each act. The best preparations, which generally render private theatricals both laborious and expensive, add but little to the pleasure of the beholders, whose attention is fixed upon the actors, and who can always see far finer scenes at a minor theatre than at any private theatricals. Were we content with greater simplicity in our amusements, how much vain ostentation, heart-sickening expense, self-recrimination, and trouble, might be avoided!

As a valid objection to private theatricals, it has been urged that they are apt to encourage a taste for the green-room of the public theatre in young men and boys; in women the risk is less, for few women are ever known to go on the stage except from necessity. I own this objection to theatricals is the greatest that can be urged. It can only be answered in mitigation that, where there exists a taste of the kind, it is better that it should be indulged at home, instead of at the theatre, with the modest inmates of a well-governed house, instead of with professional actors. Like all other amusements, the abuse is probable, but the power of restraint rests within ourselves.

Under the same head as private theatricals may come dramatised charades and proverbs, so much in fashion at the present time. These last have some great advantages over the standard plays; they are better suited to a parlour; they do not provoke comparison between the young actors, and the favourite public idols; they require but little scenery and arrangement; they are short; and they do not require so many subordinate characters.

Impromptu charades and proverbs are delightful, and are the occasion for much merriment; the mistakes, the absurd contrasts between character and costume, the scenery – a deep, hanging wood, the court of Louis Quatorze or the deck of a man of war, being improvised at a moment's notice, only add to the merry enjoyment.

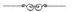

One rule you must observe if you join in these amusements: never to carry your gaiety into romping. Merry and laughing you may be, yet never forget you are a lady.

You may personate a newly-caught Irish chambermaid, use the broadest brogue, wear the commonest dress, throw yourself heartily and thoroughly into the part, losing your personal identity almost entirely, and yet you may retain that nameless charm, which will place you in the mind of each of the audience as a lady of refinement.

YOU must also be perfectly good-natured and self-sacrificing; ready to play the smallest parts with the same interest you would throw into the principal ones. Try to throw out all the good points in the parts taken by the other members of the company. If you play an insignificant part, play it well, with all the grace you can, make the most of it, but do not try to raise it to the first place. Yield gracefully the prominent position to those who claim it in the plot of the play, and never try by conspicuous dress or by play, to go beyond the position set down for you.

SMALL social gatherings will be much more entertaining, the time will pass much more quickly, and the conversation flows more freely if the fingers are employed with some light work.

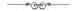

PRETTY presents – nay, beautiful ones – may be made in this way, when the fingers would otherwise be idle, and these will have an additional value in being the work of your own hands.

F ROM the most remote ages needlework has been, not only a source of pecuniary advantage for poor women, but also of pleasant pastime for the rich. It is one of the most elegant of the imitative arts, and from time immemorial it has been an amusement for otherwise idle fingers, from the cottage to the palace.

I HAVE not space for a long disquisition upon the uses and pleasures of fancy work; every woman has moments when such pretty playwork will be a valuable recreation. The taste for fancy work increases daily, and can be made not only ornamental, but useful. A ladies' wardrobe consists of so many, and such varied objects, that the evenings of an entire winter may be spent in making various useful garments, which are, at the same time, suitable for company sewing. Opera hoods, wool shawls, sleeves, Sontags, and other ladies' articles, may be varied by embroidering smoking caps, slippers, or handkerchiefs for gentlemen.

E MBROIDERING on canvas, or tapestry work, opens a large field for taste and skill in execution. Beautiful articles for presents, chair covers, sofa cushions, slippers, may be worked in the otherwise idle moments spent in familiar society, and the fingers will soon acquire skill and astonishing rapidity.

THE German ladies have constantly on hand a piece of netting or other fancy work, which they carry from place to place, and take out when conversing; and so far from entirely engrossing their thoughts, they chat more readily and freely with their fingers thus employed.

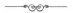

AMERICAN ladies will find the custom worth imitating. Many tedious hours will be smoothly, pleasantly passed, with the mind free, but the fingers pleasantly occupied.

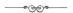

AN evening passed in sewing or knitting, with one good reader to entertain the industrious workers, will be found very pleasant. I have known a circle of young people meet every week to work in this way, the reader being changed twice or three times in the course of the evening, and these meetings have proved so pleasant, that scarcely any member failed to plead 'prior engagement' if invited out upon the evening appointed to read and sew.

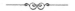

IT was formerly objected by the adversaries to mental culti- vation in women, that the acquirement of book learning would make them neglect needlework; but so far from this being the case, the present, which is often called the age of learning, is pre-eminently a working age. Never were fingers more actively engaged than those of the rising female gener- ation; braiding, embroidery, Berlin work, knitting, netting, and crochet, are all in full play. A long neglected work has been recently revived, called by the French 'La Frivolité'. It is very pretty evening work, partly because it does not impede conversation, for it may be carried on almost without looking at it, and partly because no other work shows to so much advantage the grace and delicacy of the hands. The most simple form of this work was anciently known under the name of Tatting, but that only consisted of a series of loops in a straight line, which were used for trimming linen articles, and which was not so pretty as La Frivolité, which has varieties which are a good imitation of point, and may be used for collars and sleeves.

CHAPTER XXI

Servants

AN English writer, speaking of servants, says – 'There is no question but that we should seek to perform *all* our duties without hope of recompense; and yet, as regards our treatment of servants, we should be especially careful that, in endeavouring to make their bodily comfort and mental improvement an object of consideration, we do not allow ourselves to dwell on the hope of gratitude or affection from them in return. Many have done so, and having, with that view, been tempted to accord unwise indulgences and to overlook serious faults, they have found that, far from gaining the love of their servants, they have incurred their contempt; and when they have perceived that their favours, unappreciated, have led but to new encroachments, they have hardened their hearts and rushed into an opposite extreme. Then they have considered their servants as mere machines, from which labour must be extorted by all available means.'

'THERE is one thing a manservant values beyond all that your kindness and your consideration can do for him – his liberty; liberty to eat, drink, and be merry, with your things in the company of his own friends; liberty to get the housemaid to clean his candlesticks, and bring up his coals; and the housemaid wishes for liberty to lie in bed in the morning, because she was up so late talking to John in the pantry; liberty to wear flounces and flowers. The cook desires liberty too. For this liberty, if you grant it, they will despise you; if you deny it, they will respect you. Aim at their esteem; despair of their love or gratitude; make your place what the best class of servants will value, and, though in their heart, they may not thank you for it, you will gain, perhaps, one servant out of twenty who will keep gross imposition and gross immorality at bay.'

'THESE remarks can never be intended to deny the warm attachment of female servants to the children of their employers. Deep love, no doubt, is lavished by many a woman on the babe she has nursed. There is a great deal to be said on the chapter of nurses which would require to be dealt with by itself. Much wisdom is required in the administration of a nursery, to which few general rules would apply. Cruel is the tyranny the nurse frequently practises on the parent, who often refrains from entering her nursery, not from want of love to her children, but positive dread of the sour looks which greet her. Let her be firm, let no shrinking from grieving her darling, who would "break his heart if his Nanna went", deter her from discharging the encroaching servant.'

'ON the choice of servants much of the comfort of the young housekeeper depends. It often happens that her choice has been determined by appearance rather than the value of character. If such be the case, she will have many difficulties to encounter. It is, in the present day, hardly safe to take a servant if there be a single objection to character, however it may be glossed over by the person referred to on this point; for there is now an unhealthy disposition to pass over the failings of servants who have left their places, and to make them perfect in the eyes of others. In respect to sobriety, many people will not acknowledge that a servant had had the vice of drinking, but will cover the unpleasant truth in such gentle and plausible terms that it becomes difficult to comprehend how far the hint is grounded, or not. Be assured when a lady or gentleman hesitates on this point, or on that of honesty, it is wiser not to engage a servant. Nor are you deviating from Christian charity in not overlooking a dereliction of so material a sort. The kindest plan to the vast community of domestic servants is to be rigid in all important points, and having, after a due experience, a just confidence in them, to be somewhat indulgent to errors of a more trivial nature.'

'**B**ut is it so? The beauty of everything is fitness. Is the half-fine, unladylike, yet ladylike creature, who answers to your dressing-room bell, half so respectable as the old-fashioned, plainly dressed, careful, homely maiden of your young days? Is it not with a feeling of disgust that you turn from the attempted finery, and sigh for plain collars, and caps undecked by flowers, again? I think, among the best-bred, the most sensible, and, indeed, the most highly born people of a superior stamp, this disgust is so strong that, in some families, a grave and suitable costume is introduced for the female servants, and the effect is satisfactory, both on the appearance and on the mode of thinking of these persons. But this wise, and therefore kind plan, is far from being general; and I have heard that a lady's-maid complained to her mistress that she found herself the subject of ridicule, owing to her not wearing silks, and indeed satins, as the other ladies'-maids did.'

'WHILE on the subject of servants, I must deprecate the over-indulgence of the present system towards them. Formerly they were treated with real kindness, but it was the kindness that exacted duty in return, and took a real interest in the welfare of each servant. The reciprocal tie in former times between servant and master was strong, now it is wholly gone. The easy rule of masters and mistresses proceeds far more from indifference than from kindness of heart; for the real charity is to keep servants steadily to their duties. They are a class of persons to whom much leisure is destruction; the pursuits of their idle hours are seldom advantageous to them, and theirs are not minds which can thrive in repose. Idleness, to them, is peculiarly the root of all evil, for, if their time is not spent in vicious amusements, it is often passed in slander, discontent, or vanity. In writing thus, I do not recommend a hard or inconsiderate system to servants. They require, and in many instances they merit, all that can be done to alleviate a situation of servitude. They ought not to be the slaves of caprice or the victims of temper. Their work should be measured out with a just hand; but it should be regularly exacted in as much perfection as can be expected in variable and erring human nature.'

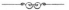

'ANOTHER point on which I would recommend firmness is that of early hours. In this respect example is as important as precept; but, however uncertain you may be yourself, I would not relax a rule of that kind. For every comfort during the day depends upon the early rising of your servants. Without this, all their several departments are hurried through or neglected in some important respect.'

'YOUR mode of address to servants must be decisive, yet mild. The authoritative tone I do not recommend. It is very unbecoming to any young person, and it rarely attains the end desired; but there is a quiet dignity of deportment which few servants ever can resist. This should be tempered with kindness, when circumstances call it forth, but should never descend to familiarity. For no caution is more truly kind than which confines servants strictly to their own sphere.'

'MUCH evil results from the tendency, more especially of very young, or of very old mistresses of families, to partiality. Commonly, one servant becomes the almost avowed favourite; and it is difficult to say whether that display of partiality is the more pernicious to the servant who is the object of it, or to the rankling and jealous minds of the rest of the household. It is true that it is quite impossible to avoid entertaining a greater degree of confidence in some servants than in others; but it should be shown with a due regard to the feelings of all. It is, of course, allowable towards those who take a decidedly responsible and confidential situation in a household. Still, never let such persons assume the reins of government; let them act the part of helmsman to the vessel, but not aspire to the control of the captain.'

'I T is generally wise and right, after a due experience of the principles and intentions of servants, to place confidence in their honesty, and to let them have the comfort of knowing that you do so. At the same time, never cease to exercise a system of supervision. The great principle of housekeeping is regularity; and without this (one of the most difficult of the minor virtues to practice) all efforts to promote order must be ineffectual. I have seen energetic women, clever and well intentioned, fail in attaining a good method, owing to their being uncertain in hours, governed by impulse, and capricious. I have seen women, inferior in capacity, slow, and apathetic, make excellent heads of families, as far as their household was concerned, from their steadiness and regularity. Their very power of enduring monotony has been favourable to their success in this way, especially if they are not called upon to act in peculiar and difficult cases, in which their actual inferiority is traceable. But these are not the ordinary circumstances of life.'

'I N closing these remarks on the management of servants, let me exhort you never to forget that they are fellow-labourers, in the life of probation, with ourselves; let us not embitter their lives by harshness, or proffer to them temptation from carelessness and over-indulgence. Since all that is given us of this world's goods is but in trust, let us regard our servants as beings for whose conduct, while under our control, we are more or less responsible. It is true that, if they come to us with morals wholly depraved, it is not likely that the most strenuous exertions can amend them; but many waver between good and evil. Let us endeavour to excite in their minds a respect for virtue, to give them motives for industry, inducements to save their wages. Those who have large households should not deem the morals of the meanest of their servants beneath their investigation, or too obscure for their influence to reach.'

WHEN opening the door some servants hold it ajar and hold a long parley with the person on the steps, as if afraid they wished to enter for the purpose of murder or theft.

TRAIN them to answer the door promptly, speak politely to anyone who may be there, excuse you, if necessary, to visitors in courteous terms, or, if you are in, show the callers into the parlour, take their card, and come back quickly with your answer.

CHAPTER XXII

On a Young Lady's Conduct When Contemplating Marriage

T HE following chapter, met with in a recent perusal of an English work for young ladies, strikes me as so admirable, and so appropriate in this place, that I quote the chapter entire:

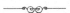

'T HE difficulties and trials of life have only just begun when a young lady fancies herself to be of sufficient importance to become the theme of animadversion. She knows little of the true importance of self-control, until she experiences the first indications of preference shown her by the other sex.'

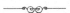

'S UCH indications are often manifested, whilst she to whom they are directed, is wholly unprepared to analyse her own feelings, before her opinions upon what she has seen are by any means developed; before she has even considered adequately, on what her happiness depends; before she has discernment to reject what is frivolous, or wisdom to prefer what is good. This is more especially the case in the highest and lowest classes, in which, by a strange analogy, they either rush into the marriage state whilst children, or wait until the bloom and hopes of youth have forever passed away, in order to form interested matches. The matured period of five-and-twenty to thirty, is passed by the lower classes in the single state in labour to gain subsistence; after thirty, or even forty, we often find them marrying. But the majority have sealed their own fate before the age of twenty.'

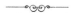

'IN high life, the same haste to dispose of daughters prevails as among the lowest classes. At seventeen, most of our belles of fashion expect to receive proposals. If they do not marry within a few years after their introduction, they have a mortified sense of having lost time – that the expectations of friends and of parents have not been fulfilled; that others have "gone off" before them. The next ten years are often a period of subdued vexation, and the sweetness and contentment of the original character is impaired. About seven or eight and twenty, the views of life are sobered – the expectations chastened – a renovation takes place – women again become agreeable; their minds must in the lapse of time, even with a miserable store of observation, have improved. They then often marry – and, if the union be not a mere effort of despair, if it be based on sound and holy principles, and on good sense, there is, for both parties engaged, a great likelihood of happiness.'

'BUT, it may be naturally contended, that there come not to *all* young ladies the opportunities of which I write; that indications of preference arrive not to all. I am inclined to believe that, with good temper, pleasing manners, and respectable connections, there exists, in modern society, very few young ladies who have not received under various circumstances, some marks of preference, more or less decided. Beauty and plainness are arbitrary, not positive, terms. Unless there be any actual deformity, any great infirmity, in which case I think it were cruel to presuppose the likelihood of such indications, there is no one, that I hardly ever met with, who has not had, on some grounds, her partisans and admirers. The plain are often particularised as elegant; tastes vary: even a sour look I have heard admired as sensible, cold manners eulogised as correct. Opinion, however it may generally verge to the correct, springs from so many sources, it is so governed by association of ideas, such trifles may guide it, that I am never surprised at the latitude given to personal encomium nor at the endless variety and incongruity of human judgement. It is well that all have a chance of being approved, admired, beloved, and it remains for them to avail themselves of those possibilities which contribute so much to happiness. For we are sympathising beings, and a law of our nature makes us look for a return of sympathy. We are sent here to form ties, and to love, and to be loved, whether the term applies to parental, or filial, or fraternal love – or whether it respects the less sure and more fitful experiences of love, in its ordinary sense.'

--------⋅◦⊙◦⋅--------

'I DO not blame the parents who instil into their children of both sexes a desire to be married. I think those who teach the young a different lesson deceive them. Marriage, with all its chances, its infelicities, its sacrifices, is seldom so infelicitous, so uncertain, so full of sacrifice, as the single state. Life must have some objects, and those objects must be progressive. The mind is happier and healthier with such interests, even if sorrow comes along with them, than in its solitude, its desolate freedom from care, when having, as the phrase is, no troubles of the conjugal sort to disturb its tranquillity. I therefore do not censure those who desire to see their daughters happily and suitably established in life. It is the indiscreet and vulgar haste, the indelicacy, the low mercenary views, and the equally low ambition to compass a splendid match, which is blameable and revolting in the parental conduct.'

'THE eyes of her family and of her young friends are upon her, when a young lady receives the first indications of preference. She is generally ashamed of it. This is the first sentiment of a modest and ingenuous mind, and it is one indication, in my opinion, of the impropriety of early marriages. Nature seems still to wish to keep the young and blushing girl apart from that connection which entails grave and arduous duties. But Nature's voice is far less often heard than that of her adversary, expediency. I must, therefore, shape my injunctions to that which exists, not to that which we would wish to exist.'

'ALMOST sinking under this painful sense of shame, this novel disturbance of her usual set of feelings, a young girl catches at the first reed to save herself from observation and detection. I mean detection of her perception of that which others may or may not see. She seizes upon ridicule. She pretends to laugh at one, whom sometimes her youthful romantic fancy dwells upon in a very different sense. She laughs at the foibles, supposed or real, of her admirer: she plays a dangerous game. If any of those to whom she imparts her witticisms are malevolently disposed or thoughtless, she runs a risk either of wounding the feelings of a man whom she does not like, or of losing the regard of one whom she might in time not only esteem, but love.'

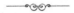

'ANOTHER effect of such attentions as awaken a consciousness in a young lady's mind, is the gratification of vanity, perhaps until then latent in her heart. The first preference is apt to upset the reason of its object as of him who shows it. The word vanity does not seem to imply danger. Vanity is generally considered an innocent failing; but it is innocent only as some kinds of food are to a healthy subject. On a weak, or even on an inexperienced mind, it acts, sometimes, fatally for the vain. A girl is either carried away by admiration so as to be flippant and foolish, or she is blinded by her vanity to the failings of the man who first admires her. She is intoxicated with the notion of an offer of marriage; she imagines, in her simplicity, effervesced as it is by the infusion of flattered vanity, that she has inspired such an attachment as will never be recovered, should she prove adverse to it. Many an engagement has been formed under this conviction, and fulfilled only to prove its fallacy, for the love which was supposed too strong to survive disappointment, has expired in the fruition of its hopes.'

'To guard against either of these risks to happiness, a well-educated girl should endeavour, in this, to exercise her judgement. She should be sincere. She is blameable to ridicule the attentions which are meant as complimentary to her. They ought to be at least regarded with respect.'

'Should they not be acceptable, she is inexcusable to requite them with levity and disdain. Let her reflect how she would like such conduct herself. Besides, she is often making a bitter enemy; perhaps she is exciting fierce and unamiable sentiments in one who otherwise might have been regarded as a mild and worthy individual. Let her be undeceived if she supposes that in thus doing she is carrying herself with dignity, or acquiring any added admiration from others. She ceases, in thus acting, to support the characteristics of a gentlewoman, which are mildness, courtesy, and reserve. If she cherishes, in spite of her pretended disgust, a secret partiality for the individual who distinguishes her, if she is lowering the esteem of a man whom she prefers, she not only incurs the hazard of losing his regard, but she is scattering ridicule on one whom she afterwards avows as her choice. In that case, she is lowering herself, or she is sowing the seeds of distrust in the minds of those who know her – she is, perhaps, frustrating and delaying her own happiness. Let her act with candour, with consideration, with good sense, and all this web which her folly would weave around her will not embarrass her. Let her not madly and obstinately resist the advice of those on whose affection to her, and on whose good judgement, experience has taught her to rely. Let her be a child in nothing except humility; let her listen to counsels; yet her own heart must decide for her – none can know so well as herself its secret throbs, or the impression of dislike or of regard which has been made upon it.'

'I AM, I confess, an enemy to trying to like a person, as I have rarely seen such a mental process end in happiness to either party. If an advantageous proposal offer itself, it is wiser decidedly to refuse it, than to trust to the slow growth of affection, upon a foundation of original dislike. And the trials of married life are such – its temptations to irritability and contention are so manifold, its anxieties so unforeseen and so complicated, that few can steer their difficult course safely and happily, unless there be a deep and true attachment, to contend with all the storms which may arise in the navigation.'

'DEEPLY impressed with this conviction, should it be the lot of any young lady in whom I were inter- ested to form a real, well-grounded attachment to a man whose circumstances were indifferent, I should counsel her, provided she can depend on the character and exertions of the object so beloved, to risk the event of an engagement – to trust to time and Providence, and to marry whenever means were afforded – convinced as I am, that patience, and trust, and true affection, raise the character, and are acceptable in the eyes of our Heavenly Father. But in such a case, she must school her mind to meet the anxieties which attend limited means. She must prepare herself, by habits of diligence and economy, to become a poor man's wife.'

'OF this let the young be assured; there are few situations in life, in which a man, young, and in health, cannot meliorate his circumstances, if he possess energy and if he be stimulated by a true affection. The clergyman, with humble stipend, often hopeless from want of interest, has leisure – he has had education. He may, if he desires to assist himself, have recourse to literary labour, or to tuition. If he make not such exertion, during the course of an engagement, what hope can there be of him in future life?'

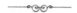

'THE young lawyer, however tedious his advancement, however few his opportunities, may also distinguish himself in a literary career. Innumerable are the subjects open to one of such a profession. How few avail themselves of the chance! Upon this rely, the man truly in love will make the effort. To the military man, though perhaps he may be less qualified, the same course is open, in a degree. Some of our best travels, some of our most amusing literary productions, have been the compositions of military men. And the advantage of this mode of aiding a small fortune is, that a man not only does not lower, but he raises his position by it, if his works are moral, written in a gentlemanly spirit, and affording information. However deep the attachment, however agreeable the object, if a man be indisposed to help himself to independence and competence, I should counsel no woman to continue an engagement formed in the expectation of "times mending". When I advocate the indulgence of attachment, it is to worthy, not to unworthy, objects.'

'WITH every vigilance, with little to blame, little to repent, such cases will occur in this world. The feelings are interested, but the judgement distrusts. Happy is it for those who know the combat between affection and principle only in single life, and have not the misery of encountering so severe a destiny when it can no longer be remedied – who know not how to fulfil the vow to honour what is proved to be unworthy – and yet still must love – for the affections once given, are little in our own power.'

'IN such a case occurring to the young, in, perhaps, a first attachment, I think they must be guided by friends. I am *not* an advocate for the interference of friends: where it is much a question of a long and contingent engagement – a question of being married at once, or of waiting, in some uncertainty – a question of ease or discomfort, of limited means or luxury – in such instances, if the moral character be unexceptionable, it is the duty of parents to point out all the risk, all the disadvantages, but to leave the heart to form its own decisions. Let them not seek to wrench the affections from the channel in which they flowed, when fresh from their source. They cannot know how deep the channel is – they cannot know if ever those pure and beautiful waters will flow in peace again when once hastily turned aside. But in cases of moral character, of right or wrong, the affair is wholly different, and the strictest parental authority ought, upon due enquiry, to be exercised.'

'AVOID young persons of your own age. If possible, except to a sister, whose deep interest in you will probably teach her a superior lesson, never confide in young friends, a similar trial as that to which I have referred. In general, your resolution will be weakened, your feelings re-excited, your confidence in your best advisers will be shaken. For the young usually take the part of the rejected lover – they delight in that dangerous species of sympathy which flatters with hope. They are naturally incredulous as to the delinquencies of a man who is agreeable, and in love; they incline to the notion of the hard-heartedness of fathers, uncles, and elder brothers; and even, if they happen to possess good sense, or to exercise the rare quality of prudence in such matters, the very communication of any sorrow, or the recital of any feelings, gives not only a merely temporary relief, but deadens that sorrow and strengthens those feelings, which grow every time they are imparted.'

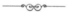

'I WOULD, on many grounds, caution the young against hasty engagements. It seems extraordinary that the welfare of a life should often be determined upon the acquaintance of a few weeks. The principles, it is true, may be ascertained from the knowledge of others, the manners may please, the means and expectations may all be clearly understood. But the temper – that word of unspeakable import – the daily habits, the power of constancy – these are not to be known without a long and severe examination of the motives, and a daily observation of the conduct, of others. Very little suffices to mar the happiness of married life, if that little proceed in the character of a man, from a rooted selfishness.'

CHAPTER XXIII

Bridal Etiquette

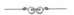

I N preparing a bridal outfit, it is best to furnish the wardrobe for at least two years, in underclothes, and one year in dresses, though the bonnet and cloak, suitable for the coming season, are all that are necessary, as the fashions in these articles change so rapidly. If you are going to travel, have a neat dress and cloak of some plain colour, and a close bonnet and veil. Avoid, as intensely vulgar, any display of your position as a *bride*, whilst travelling.

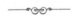

T AKE, first, the weddings at church. In this case none are invited to the ceremony excepting the family, and the reception is at the house of the bride's mother, or nearest relative, either on the wedding day or upon her return from the bridal tour.

I N sending out the invitations, let the card of the bride-groom and that of the bride be tied together with a white ribbon, and folded in the note paper upon which is printed the name of the bride's mother, with the date of the reception day, thus –

Mrs John Saunders.
At home, Thursday, Oct. 16th,
from 11 till 2.

No. 218, - st.

———•◦◉◦•———

OF course the hours and dates vary, but the form is the same.

———•◦◉◦•———

IF there is no bridal reception upon the wedding day, the cards are worded –

Mr and Mrs James Smith.
At home, Wednesdays,
On, and after, June 6th.

No. 17, - st.

———•◦◉◦•———

TIE the card with the bride's maiden name upon it to this one.

———•◦◉◦•———

ENCLOSE the invitation in a white envelope, and tie it with white satin ribbon. If you send cake, have it put in a white box, and place the note outside the cover, tying it fast with white satin ribbon.

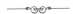

THE bride's dress must be of white entirely. If she is married in the morning, a plain white silk, white mantle, and white bonnet, full trimmed with orange flowers, with a plain veil, is the most suitable dress, and she may wear a richer one at her reception, when she returns from her bridal tour.

AS soon as the carriages come, let the bridesmaids, and relatives set off first. Last, the bride with her parents. The bride, her parents, and the bridesmaids go immediately to the vestry, where they meet the bridegroom, and the groomsmen. The father of the bride gives her his arm and escorts her to the altar, the bridegroom walking on the other side. Then follow the bridesmaids and groomsmen in couples.

WHEN they reach the altar the bridegroom removes his right hand glove, but the bride keeps hers on until the clergyman takes the ring. The first bridesmaid then removes the left hand glove, and it is not resumed. The bridesmaids should wear white dresses, white mantles, and bonnets, but not veils or orange flowers.

I F there is a breakfast or morning reception, the bride will not change her dress until she retires to put on her travelling attire. If the wedding takes place in the evening at church, to be followed by a full dress reception at home, the bride should wear a white lace dress over satin, or any other material to suit her own taste, a veil, falling from her head to her feet, fastened to the hair by a coiffure of orange flowers; white kid gloves, and white satin slippers. A bouquet, if carried, should contain only white flowers.

T HE bridesmaids may wear white, or some thin, light-coloured material over white, a headdress of flowers, and carry bouquets of mixed flowers.

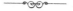

A FTER the ceremony is over, the parents of the bride speak to her first; then her near relatives, and not until then the other members of the company.

——————

I T is not usual now to have dancing, or even music, at a wedding, and the hour is named upon the cards, at which the guests are expected to retire.

——————

A VERY pretty effect is produced in the wedding group, if the bride wears pure white, and the bridesmaids white, with flowers and trimmings of a different colour. Thus, one in white, with a headdress and trimming of green leaves; another, white, with blue ribbons and forget-me-nots; another, white, with pink roses and ribbons.

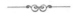

L ET the supper be laid early, and ready when the ceremony is over, that the guests may pass into the dining room, if they wish, as soon as they have spoken to the bride. If a morning wedding, let the table be set as for an evening wedding.

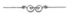

A T parties given to a newly married couple, the brides- maids and groomsmen are always invited, and the whole party are expected to wear the same dresses as at the wedding.

CHAPTER XXIV

————⚬⟨⟩⚬————

Hints on Health

T HE universal remark of travellers visiting America, as well as the universal complaint of Americans themselves, relates to the ill health of the fairer portion of the community. Look where you will, go to any city in the vast Union, the remark and complaint will be made everywhere. With every natural advantage of climate, yet from North to South, East to West the cry resounds.

————⚬⟨⟩⚬————

F OREIGNERS, admiring the dark-eyed girls of the southern states or the blondes of the northern ones, will remark, with comments upon beauty – 'But she looks delicate, poor thing! – Not strong? Ah! I thought not, none of the American women are, and how soon these young beauties fade!'

————⚬⟨⟩⚬————

'L IGHT and sunshine are needful for your health. Get all you can; keep your windows clean. Do not block them up with curtains, plants, or bunches of flowers; these last poison the air, in small rooms.'

'FRESH air is needful for your health. As often as you can, open all your windows, if only for a short time in bad weather; in fine weather, keep them open, but never sit in draughts. When you get up, open the windows wide, and throw down the bedclothes, that they may be exposed to fresh air some hours, daily, before they are made up. Keep your bedclothes clean; hang them to the fire when you can. Avoid wearing at night what you wear in the day. Hang up your day-clothes at night. Except in the severest weather, in small, crowded sleeping-rooms, a little opening at the top of the window-sash is very important; or you will find one window pane of perforated zinc very useful. You will not catch cold half so easily by breathing pure air at night. Let not the beds be directly under the windows. Sleeping in exhausted air creates a desire for stimulants.'

'PURE water is needful for your health. Wash your bodies as well as your faces, rubbing them all over with a coarse cloth. If you cannot wash thus every morning, pray do so once a week. Crying and cross children are often pacified by a gentle washing of their little hands and faces – it soothes them. Babies' heads should be washed carefully, every morning with soap. No scurf should be suffered to remain upon them. Get rid of all slops and dirty water at once. Disease, and even death, is often the consequence of our own negligence. Wash your rooms and passages at least once a week, use plenty of clean water; but do not let your children stay in them while they are wet, it may bring on croup or inflammation of the chest.'

'WHOLESOME food is needful for your health. Buy the most strengthening. Pieces of fresh beef and mutton go the farthest. Eat plenty of fresh salt with food; it prevents disease. Pray do not let your children waste their pennies in tarts, cakes, bull's eyes, hardbake, sour fruit, etc., they are very unwholesome, and hurt the digestion. People would often, at twenty years of age, have a nice little sum of money to help them on in the world, if they had put in the savings' bank the money so wasted; cocoa is cheaper and much more nourishing than *tea*. None of these liquids should be taken *hot*, but lukewarm; when hot they inflame the stomach, and produce indigestion.'

LET it not be supposed that it is not the duty of every young lady to take due care of her health, and to preserve in all its power of utility every portion of vigour which has been bestowed on her.

WITH many young ladies, it appears to be a maxim to do everything in their power to destroy the health which is so much wanted in the real business of life, and which forms so important a requisite to happiness. In the first place, as to hours – they never leave the ballroom until utterly exhausted, and scarcely fit to crawl to bed. The noon-day sleep, the scarcely touched breakfast, that most important meal, are followed by preparations for the succeeding night's pleasures, or in head-aching morning calls, driving about in a close carriage, or lounging on a sofa, in an overheated room, reading novels.

D RESSING follows; the warm wrapper or dress is thrown aside; over the tightly drawn corsets is fastened a flimsy dress, with an inch of sleeve; the neck laid bare; thin stockings drawn on, in place of thick ones, and the consumption-seeker goes forth to the ballroom again.

'I NFLUENZA has been long known in the world. It has often visited Europe; and made its appearance on our shores with greater severity than at present. It has sometimes been very severe, and left many persons ill for a year or two.'

'T HE symptoms of influenza need not be dwelt on, as they have been so generally felt by our readers or their friends. It varies in different people, to be sure, both in kind and in degree. Considering the number of people it attacks, it may be looked on as an innocent disease; but, on the other hand, looking at the increase it has made in the number of deaths, it is an exceedingly serious one after all.'

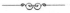

'I N simple cases – confinement to a pure and temperate air, warm drinks, and a warm bath, or, at least, a warm foot-bath, with an extra blanket, and a little more rest than usual, keeping to mild food, and toast and water, and taking, if necessary, a dose of aperient medicine, is all that is required. In serious cases, the domestic treatment must become professional. Mustard plasters to the back relieve the headache. Squills find other medicines "loosen" the outstanding cough. Bark and wine, and even cold baths are sometimes requisite for the weakness left behind. But these things can only be used with discrimination by a regular professional man.'

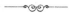

'THE duration of sleep should not, in the adult, exceed six or eight hours; women injure their health greatly by excess in this respect. On rising, all women should use some mode of cold or tepid bath; and, indeed, in this respect the practice of the present day is admirable; there is every facility for the bath. To some, the use of the shower-bath is deleterious, and to all inconvenient, and not likely to be resorted to except when positively ordered. Dr Combe recommends for *general* use the tepid or warm bath, as being much more suitable than the cold bath, "especially in the winter for those who are not robust, and full of animal heat".'

'IN the formation of those habits which are necessary for the preservation of health, another circumstance, which, from its importance to health, cannot be deemed trifling should be mentioned. It is a general practice that beds should be made as soon as the occupants have left their rooms, and before the air has been freely admitted to play upon the recent depositary of the human frame; but this should be avoided. The bed-linen and blankets should be taken off, and the windows opened, so that, for an hour or more, a thorough ventilation should be procured.'

'UPON another point, the inconsistency and mental blindness of women are almost inconceivable – the insufficiency of their dress to resist the attacks of our variable climate. How few women clothe themselves like rational beings! Although, in latter years, they have wisely adopted the use of warm dresses, and, more especially, of the valuable Scottish plaid, yet how commonly they neglect the aid of flannel in preserving them not only from cold, but in securing a necessary circulation of vitality in the skin! "The necessary effect of deficient circulation in the skin," remarks Dr Combe, "is to throw a disproportionate mass of blood inwards; and when this condition exists, insufficient clothing perpetuates the evil, until internal disease is generated, and health is irrecoverably lost."'

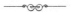

'BUT, whilst insufficiency of clothing is to be deprecated, excessive wrapping up should also be avoided. Great differences exist between the power of generating heat and resisting cold in individuals, and it is therefore impossible to prescribe general rules upon the subject of clothing. The best maxim is, not to dress in an invariable way in all cases, but to put on clothing sufficient in the individual case, to protect the body effectively against the sensation of cold.'

'THE insufficiency of warmth in the clothing of females constitutes only one part of its injurious effects. The tightness of dress obstructs the insensible perspiration hurtfully, and produces an irregular circulation. Every part and function of the human frame are linked together so closely, that we cannot act wrongly towards one organ without all suffering, nor act rightly without all sharing the benefit of our judgement and good sense.'

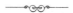

'THE mischief arising from cold or wet feet is admitted by all persons who have given the subject of health even the most casual consideration. In conversing with very aged people, you will generally find a disregard of diet, and very different notions and practices upon the subject of exercise and ablution; but they all agree in the necessity of keeping the feet dry. I remember enquiring of a venerable clergyman, who, up to the age of ninety-six, had enjoyed a fair proportion of health, after a youth of delicacy. I asked him what system he pursued. "Now," was his reply, "I never took much care what I ate; I have always been temperate. I never minded the weather; but I always took care to keep my feet dry and well shod." Wet and damp are, indeed, more unwholesome when applied to the feet than when they affect other parts; "because they receive a greater supply of blood to carry on a high degree of perspiration, and because their distance from the heart, or centre of circulation, diminishes the force with which this is carried on, and thus leaves them more susceptible from external causes."'

'Goo, in his infinite benevolence, has given to his creatures other means of acquiring a healthy warmth than by clothing; he has endowed us with the power of exercise – that blessing which women of weak judgement and indolent natures are so prone to neglect and disparage. Most ladies appear to think that the privilege of walking is only intended for persons of inferior condition. They busy themselves, in their indoor occupations all the morning, take a hearty luncheon, and drive out in their carriages until dinnertime. It is partly owing to such customs as these that a rapid deterioration takes place in the physical state of our sex, in their looks, and in their power of utility, and enjoyment of happiness. God never intended us to be inactive.'

'The chief purpose of the muscles with which we are endowed, is to enable us to carry into effect the volitions of the mind; and, whilst fulfilling this grand object, the active exercise of the muscles is conducive to the well-being of many other important functions. The processes of digestion, respiration, secretion, absorption, and nutrition, are promoted, and the healthful condition of the whole body influenced. The mind also is depressed or exhilarated by the proper or improper use of muscular exercise; for man is intended for a life of activity: nor can his functions ever go on so properly as when he duly exercises those organs with which Nature has endowed him. The evils arising from want of exercise are numerous: the circulation, from the absence of due stimulus, becomes languid, the appetite and digestion are weakened, the respiration is imperfect, and the blood becomes so ill-conditioned, that when distributed through the body it is inadequate to communicate the necessary stimulus to healthy and vigorous action.'

'OF all modes of exercise, that which nature has bestowed upon us, walking, is decidedly the most salutary; and the prevailing system of substituting horse and carriage exercise almost entirely for it, is far from being advantageous to the present generation. Walking, which has for its aim some pleasing pursuit, and, therefore, animates the mind, is efficacious to the majority. Gardening, which is a modification of walking, offers many advantages both to the delicate and the strong, and it is a species of exercise which we can adjust to our powers. In a continued walk you must go on – you must return; there is no appeal, even if you have gone too far, and would willingly give up any further exertion. But, while gardening, you are still at home – your exertions are devoted to objects the most interesting, because progressive; hope and faith form a part of your stimulus. The happy future, when flowers shall bloom around you, super-sedes in your thoughts the vexatious present or the mournful past. About you are the budding treasures of spring, or the gorgeous productions of summer, or the rich hues of those beauties which autumn pours forth most lavishly before it departs – and is succeeded by winter.'

'DANCING, which is the most frequent mode of exercise with ladies in great cities, practised, as it is, in heated rooms, and exhausting from its violence, often does more harm than good, from producing languor and over-fatigue. Unhappily there are but few modes of exercise indoors adapted for women. If, from any circumstances, they are confined to their homes, and they become feverish and languid from want of exercise, it never occurs to them to throw open the windows and to walk about, or to make use of battledore and shut-tlecock, or any other mode of exertion. They continue sitting, reading, or walking, or lounging, or sleeping, or gossiping – whilst the bloom of health is rapidly giving place to the wanness and debility of the imprisoned frame.'

CHAPTER XXV

Miscellaneous

THERE are many little pieces of rudeness, only too common, which, while they evince ill-breeding, and are many of them extremely annoying, yet they are met with every day, and in persons otherwise well bred.

AS they come under no particular head, they will merely be mentioned here, as habits carefully to avoid.

IT is rude to look over the shoulder of a person who is either reading or writing, yet it is done every day.

———

TO stand with the arms akimbo, the hands on the hips, or with the arms crossed, while conversing, is exceedingly unladylike.

———

A void restless movements either with the hands, or feet; to sit perfectly quiet, without stiffness, easily, yet at the same time almost motionless, is one of the surest proofs of high-breeding.

A void passing before persons seated in the same room with yourself. If you must rise to move from place to place, endeavour to pass behind the chairs of your companions. Above all, never pass between two persons who are conversing together.

I f you meet a gentleman at the foot of a flight of stairs, do not go up before him. Stop, bow, and motion to him to precede you. He will return your bow, and run up, leaving you to follow him.

A ccepting presents from gentlemen is a dangerous thing. It is better to avoid any such obligations, and, if you make it a rule *never* to accept such presents, you will avoid hurting anyone's feelings, and save yourself from all further perplexity.

I n meeting your elderly friends in the street, look at them long enough to give them an opportunity of recognising you; and if they do so, return their salutations respectfully, not with the familiar nod you would give to one of your own age.

NEVER refuse a request or invitation in order to be urged, and accept afterwards. Comply at once. If the request is sincere, you will thus afford gratification; if not, the individual making it deserves to be punished for insincerity, by being taken at her word.

IT is not polite when asked what part of a dish you will have, to say, 'Any part – it is quite indifferent to me'; it is hard enough to carve for one's friends, without choosing for them.

IT is not polite for married ladies to talk, in the presence of gentlemen, of the difficulty they have in procuring domestics, and how good-for-nothing they are when procured.

IT is not polite to put food upon the plate of a guest without asking leave, or to press her to eat more than she wants.

NEVER affect a foolish reserve in a mixed company, keeping aloof from others as if in a state of mental abstraction. If your brain is so full and so busy that you cannot attend to the little civilities, cheerful chit-chat, and light amusements of society, keep out of it.

———❦———

NEVER read in company. You may open a book to look over the engravings, if you will, but do not attend to the letter-press until you are alone.

———❦———

MANY persons, whose tongues never utter a scandalous word, will, by a significant glance, a shrug of the shoulders, a sneer, or curl of the lip, really make more mischief, and suggest harder thoughts than if they used the severest language. This is utterly detestable. If you have your tongue under perfect control, you can also control your looks, and you are cowardly, contemptible, and wicked, when you encourage and countenance slander by a look or gesture.

———❦———

NEVER speak of gentlemen by their first name unless you are related to them. It is very unladylike to use the surname, without the prefix, Mr. To hear a lady speak of Smith, Brown, Anderson, instead of Mr Anderson or Mr Smith sounds extremely vulgar, and is a mark of low breeding.

———❦———

AVOID eccentricity either in dress, conversation, or manner. It is a form of vanity, as it will attract attention, and is therefore in bad taste.

———❦———

NEVER act as if in a hurry. Ease of action need not imply laziness, but simply polite self-possession.

———⚬◦⦿◦⚬———

NOTHING but a quick perception of the feelings of others, and a ready sympathy with them, can regulate the thousand little proprieties that belong to visits of condolence and congratulation. There is one hint, however, as regards the former, which may perhaps be useful, and that is, not to touch upon the cause of affliction, unless the mourner leads the way to it; and if a painful effort is made to appear cheerful, and to keep aloof from the subject, do not make the slightest allusion that could increase this feeling.

———⚬◦⦿◦⚬———

NEVER put temptation in a servant's way; never be severe for trifling offences, such as accidentally breaking anything, but reserve your severity for those offences which are moral evils, such as a want of truth, general laxity of principle, etc. The orders given to servants should be clear and definite; and they should be trained as much as possible to perform their duties regularly, so that every morning they may know pretty nearly what will be expected of them during the day. It is a great point to live, when you are alone, as if you expected company; that is to say, to have everything so neat and orderly that you need not be ashamed of anyone seeing your table. It is very little more trouble, and certainly no more expense; and the advantages in point of comfort are unspeakable.

———⚬◦⦿◦⚬———

I F a foolish girl, by dint of squeezing and bracing with busk and bones, secures the conventional beauty of a wasp waist, she is tolerably certain to gain an addition she by no means bargained for, a *red nose*, which, in numberless instances, is produced by no other cause than the unnatural girth, obstructing circulation, and causing stagnation of the blood, in that prominent and important feature. Often, in assemblages of the fair, we have seen noses faultless in form, but tinged with the abhorred hue, to which washes and cosmetics have been applied in wild despair; but in vain! If the lovely owners had known the cause, how speedily the effect would have vanished! for surely the most perverse admirer of a distorted spine and compressed lungs, would deem the acquisition of a dram-drinker's nose too heavy a condition to be complied with.

A WELL-BRED person will take care not to use slang words and expressions. There never has been a time, at least in late years, when there have not been some two or three cant vulgarisms in vogue among all the blackguards of the country. Sometimes these phrases have been caught up from some popular song or farce; sometimes, we believe, they have had their origin 'where assembles the collective wisdom of the country'. A dozen of these terse but meaningless sayings now dance before our recollection, for who has not heard them, even to loathing? But from whatever source they may have been drawn, or whatever wit there might be in their original position, the obtrusion of them into decent society is an unwarrantable piece of impertinence.

WITH regard to any specific rules for dressing, we do not pretend to arbitrate in such matters. Let a true sense of propriety, of the fitness of things, regulate all your habits of living and dressing, and it will produce such a beautiful harmony and consistency of character as will throw a charm around you that all will feel, though few may comprehend. Always consider well whether the articles of dress, which you wish to purchase, are suited to your age, your condition, your means; to the climate, to the particular use to which you mean to put them; and let the principles of good taste keep you from the extremes of the fashion, and regulate the form, so as to combine utility and beauty, whilst the known rules of harmony in colours save you from shocking the eye of the artist by incongruous mixtures.

'MANNERS,' says the eloquent Edmund Burke, 'are of more importance than laws. Upon them, in a great measure, the laws depend. The law can touch us here and there, now and then. Manners are what vex or sooth, corrupt or purify, exalt or debase, barbarise or refine, by a constant, steady, uniform, insensible operation, like that of the air we breathe in. They give their whole form and colours to our lives. According to their quality they aid morals, they supply them, or they totally destroy them.'

FOUR IMPORTANT RULES

'ORDER is heaven's first law.'

1

*A suitable place for everything,
and everything in its place.*

2

*A proper time for everything,
and everything done in its time.*

3

*A distinct name for everything,
and everything called by its name.*

4

*A certain use for everything,
and everything put to its use.*

MUCH time would be saved; many disputes avoided; numerous articles kept from being lost or injured, and constant confusion and disorder prevented, by the strict observance of these four important rules.

———❦———

D EPEND upon it, silvery hair is better adapted to the faded cheeks of middle age, than are tresses of nut-brown or coal-black, or any of the mysterious shades produced by a dirty decoction called hair-dye.

———❦———

I F you are not quite certain of the line between neatness and the reverse, be over-scrupulous about your undergarments. The edge of a soiled petticoat, or the glimpse of a rent stocking is singularly disenchanting.

———❦———

M EN of sense – I speak not of boys of eighteen to five and twenty, during their age of detestability – men who are worth the trouble of falling in love with, and the fuss and inconvenience, of being married to, and to whom one might, after some inward conflicts, and a course perhaps of fasting and self-humiliation, submit to fulfil those ill-contrived vows of obedience which are exacted at the altar, such men want, for their wives, companions, not dolls; and women who would suit such men are just as capable of loving fervently, deeply, as the Ringlettina, full of song and sentiment, who cannot walk, cannot rise in the morning, cannot tie her bonnet-strings, faints if she has to lace her boots, never in her life brushed out her beautiful hair, would not for the world prick her delicate finger with plain sewing; but who can work harder than a factory girl upon a lamb's-wool shepherdess, dance like a dervish at balls, ride like a fox-hunter, and, whilst every breath of air gives her cold in her father's house, and she cannot think how people can endure this climate, she can go out to parties in February and March, with an inch of sleeve and half-a-quarter of bodice.

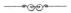

THE best way to overcome the selfishness and rudeness you sometimes meet with on public occasions, is, by great politeness and disinterestedness on your part; overcome evil with good, and you will satisfy your own conscience, and, perhaps, touch theirs. Contending for your rights stirs up the selfish feelings in others; but a readiness to yield them awakens generous sentiments, and leads to mutual accommodation. The more refined you are, and the greater have been your advantages, the more polite and considerate you should be toward others, the more ready to give place to some poor, uneducated girl, who knows no better than to push herself directly in your way.

OF late years, the wearing of jewellery, in season and out of season, both by matrons and unmarried females, has increased vastly. It is an indication that the growing wealth of the people is not accompanied by a corresponding refinement; but that the love of vulgar show, the low pride of ostentation, takes the place of a pure and elevated taste. The emulation with fashionable dames, nowadays, so far from being, as with the Spartan women, to excel each other in household virtues, is to wear the largest diamonds. And, in this ambition, they forget fitness, beauty, taste, everything but the mere vulgar desire to shine. To be gracefully and elegantly attired, in short, is secondary to the desire to be a sort of jeweller's walking show-card. We do not oppose the use of diamonds and pearls altogether, as some persons might imagine from these remarks. A few diamonds, judiciously worn, look well, on proper occasions, on married women. But young girls rarely, or never, improve their appearance by the use of these dazzling jewels; and, as a general rule, the simpler the costume of a woman in her teens, the better.

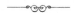

A KNOWLEDGE of domestic duties is beyond all price to a woman. Every one of the sex ought to know how to sew, and knit, and mend, and cook, and superintend a household. In every situation of life, high or low, this sort of knowledge is of great advantage. There is no necessity that the gaining of such information should interfere with intellectual acquirement or even elegant accomplishment. A well-regulated mind can find time to attend to all. When a girl is nine or ten years old, she should be accustomed to take some regular share in household duties, and to feel responsible for the manner in which her part is performed – such as her own mending, washing the cups and putting them in place, cleaning silver, or dusting and arranging the parlour.

I T is too much the fashion, in conversation, to use exaggerated expressions which are opposed to *truth*, without the person employing them being aware of it, from the mere force of habit. Why need we say splendid for pretty, magnificent for handsome, horrid for unpleasant, immense for large, thousands, or myriads, for any number more than two? This practice is pernicious, for the effect is to deprive the person who is guilty of it, from being believed, when she is in earnest. No one can trust the testimony of an individual who, in common conversation, is indifferent to the import, and regardless of the value of words.

POLITENESS is very essential to the right transaction of that great business of woman's life, *shopping*. The variety afforded by the shops of a city renders people difficult to please; and the latitude they take in examining and asking the price of goods, which they have no thought of buying, is so trying to the patience of those who attend upon them, that nothing but the most perfect courtesy of demeanour can reconcile them to it. Some persons behave, in shopping, as if no one had any rights, or any feelings, but the purchasers; as if the sellers of goods were mere automatons, put behind the counter to do their bidding; they keep them waiting, whilst they talk of other things, with a friend; they call for various goods, ask the price, and try to cheapen them, without any real intention of buying. A lady who wants decision of character, after hesitating and debating, till the poor trader's patience is almost exhausted, will beg him to send the article to her house, for her to examine it there; and, after giving him all this trouble, she will refuse to purchase it, without any scruple or apology. Some think they have a right to exchange articles at the place where they were bought; whereas that privilege should be asked as a favour, only by a good customer – and then but rarely.

CHAPTER XXVI

Recipes for the Complexion

COLD CREAM

Take 2½ ounces of sweet oil of almonds, 3 drachms of white wax, and the same of spermaceti, 2½ ounces of rose water, 1 drachm of oil of bergamot, and 15 drops each of oil of lavender, and attar of roses. Melt the wax and spermaceti in the oil of almonds, by placing them together in a jar, which should be plunged into boiling water. Heat a mortar (which should, if possible, be *marble*) by pouring boiling water into it, and letting it remain there until the mortar is uniformly heated; the water is to be poured away, and the mortar dried well. Pour the melted wax and spermaceti into the warm mortar, and add rose water gradually, while the mixture is constantly stirred or whisked with an egg-whisk, until the whole is cold, and, when nearly finished, add the oils and attar of roses.

In the absence of a mortar, a basin plunged into another containing boiling water will answer the purpose.

To soften the Skin, and improve the Complexion.

I F flowers of sulphur be mixed in a little milk, and, after standing an hour or two, the milk (without disturbing the sulphur) be rubbed into the skin, it will keep it soft, and make the complexion clear. It is to be used before washing.

Pastes

ALMOND

Take 1 ounce of bitter almonds, blanch and pound them to a fine powder, then add 1 ounce of barley flour, and make it into a smooth paste by the addition of a little honey. When this paste is laid over the skin, particularly where there are freckles, it makes it smooth and soft.

AMERICAN COSMETIC POWDER

Calcined magnesia applied the same as ordinary toilette powders, by means of a swan's-down ball, usually called a 'puff'.

CRÈME DE L'ENCLOS

Take 4 ounces of milk, 1 ounce of lemon juice, and 2 drachms of spirit of wine. Simmer over a slow fire, and then bring it to the boil, skim off the scum, and when cold apply it to the skin.

It is much used by some persons to remove freckles and sun-burnings

———◦◦◦———

Washes and Lotions

MILK OF ROSES

Take 2 ounces of blanched almonds, 12 ounces of rose water, 2 drachms each of white soft-soap (or Windsor soap), white wax, and oil of almonds, 3 ounces of rectified spirit, 1 drachm of oil of bergamot, 15 drops of oil of lavender, 8 drops of attar of roses. Beat the almonds well, and then add the rose water gradually so as to form an emulsion, mix the soap, white wax, and oil together, by placing them in a covered jar upon the edge of the fireplace, then rub this mixture in a mortar with the emulsion. Strain the whole through very fine muslin, and add the essential oils, previously mixed with the spirit.

This is an excellent wash for 'sunburns', freckles, or for cooling the face and neck, or any part of the skin to which it is applied.

———◦◦◦———

CURE FOR CHAPPED HANDS

Take 3 drachms of gum camphor, 3 drachms of white beeswax, 3 drachms of spermaceti, 2 ounces of olive oil – put them together in a cup upon the stove, where they will melt slowly and form a white ointment in a few minutes. If the hands be affected, anoint them on going to bed, and put on a pair of gloves. A day or two will suffice to heal them.

For the Teeth

TO REMOVE TARTAR FROM THE TEETH

The use of the toothbrush night and morning, and, at least, rinsing the mouth after every meal at which animal food is taken.

Once daily run the brush lightly two or three times over soap, then dip it in salt, and with it clean the teeth, working the brush up and down rather than – or as well as – backwards and forwards. This is a cheap, safe, and effectual dentrifice.

Eat freely of common cress, the sort used with mustard, under the name of small salad; it must be eaten with salt only. If thus used two or three days in succession it will effectually loosen tartar, even of long standing. The same effect is produced, though perhaps not in an equal degree, by eating strawberries and raspberries, especially the former. A leaf of common green sage rubbed on the teeth is useful both in cleansing and polishing, and probably many other common vegetable productions also.

Care of the Teeth

The water with which the teeth are cleansed should be what is called lukewarm. They should be well but gently brushed both night and morning; the brush should be neither too hard nor too soft. The best tooth-powders are made from cuttlefish, prepared chalk, and orris-root commingled together in equal quantities.

A Cheap But Good Tooth-Powder

Cut a slice of bread as thick as may be, into squares, and burn in the fire until it becomes charcoal, after which pound in a mortar, and sift through a fine muslin; it is then ready for use.

For the Hair

LOSS OF HAIR

The most simple remedy for loss of hair, is friction to the scalp of the head, using for the purpose an old toothbrush, or one of which the bristles have been softened by soaking in boiling water. The shape of the instrument adapts it to be inserted readily and effectually between the hair, where it should be rubbed backwards and forwards over the space of an inch or so at a time. In addition to the friction, which should be used once or twice a day, the head may be showered once a day with cold water, carefully drying it with soft, spongy towels.

HAIR OILS, ETC.

When used moderately, oils, ointments, etc., tend to strengthen the hair, especially when it is naturally dry. When used in excess, however, they clog the pores, prevent the escape of the natural secretions, and cause the hair to wither and fall off. The varieties of 'oils', 'greases', 'ointments', rivalling each other in their high-sounding pretensions, which are daily imposed upon public credulity, are interminable. We add one or two of the most simple.

For the Lips

ROSE LIP SALVE

8 ounces sweet almond oil, 4 ounces prepared mutton suet, 1½ ounces white wax, 2 ounces spermaceti, 20 drops attar; steep a small quantity of alkanet root in the oil, and strain before using. Melt the suet, wax, and spermaceti together, then add the coloric oil and attar.

SUPERIOR LIP SALVE

White wax, two and a half ounces; three quarters of an ounce of spermaceti, four ounces of oil of almonds. Mix well together, and apply a little to the lips at night.

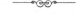

ANOTHER

A dessert spoonful of salad oil in a saucer, hold it over a candle, and drop melted wax over it till the oil is thinly covered, when they are incorporated, pour it into boxes. (Wax taper will do.)

Perfumes

To make Eau de Cologne

Four pints of rectified spirits of wine, one ounce of oil of bergamot, half an ounce of oil of lemon, half a drachm of oil of rosemary, three quarters of a drachm oil of neroli, one drachm of oil of English lavender, one drachm of oil of oranges. Mix well and then filter. If these proportions are too large, smaller ones may be used.

Eau de Cologne

Twelve drops each of oil of neroli, citron, bergamot, orange, and rosemary, one drachm of cardamom seeds, one pint of spirits of wine. Let it stand for a week.

Lavender Water

2 drachms of oil of lavender, ½ drachm of oil of bergamot, 1 drachm of essence of musk, 13 ounces of spirits of wine, 5 ounces of water. Let it stand for a week.

Also in this series

THE
GENTLEMEN'S
BOOK OF
ETIQUETTE
AND MANUAL OF
POLITENESS

£7.99 · CECIL B. HARTLEY

What do you do in polite society if you find an insect in your food?

How should a gentleman ask a lady to dance?

And what on earth is the etiquette for smoking cigars?

Ever found yourself baffled by such delicate questions of etiquette? Do not fret, for this gentlemen's guide will provide the answer to these conundrums and many more.

So when you retire to the drawing room with your port after supper, be sure to settle down with this indispensable volume full of advice for the discerning gentleman.

HESPERUS PRESS • 28 Mortimer Street, London, W1W 7RD
• T: 0207 436 0869 • www.hesperuspress.com

HESPERUS